To Jocelyn.

    May the Lord use this book to enhance your studies and relationships

        Brad Jacoby

        Dec 3, 2010

The Death of
Hip Hop, Marriage & Morals

By Brady Goodwin Jr.

The 1ST Book in the MOREality series - Connecting Hip Hop to History and the Hereafter

Self Published through
Urbanremixproject.com

Printed in the United States of America by Createspace

Cover design: Judeus Samson | coroflot.com/judeussamson

Edited by: Jezeray Weiderman; Natalie Reeves

ISBN 10 - 061537896X

ISBN 13 - 978-0-615-37896-1

To all who know, believe or simply hope that we were made for MORE

Contents

Part Three (Ethics): Immoral Mortals & The Moral Immortal

Part One

*N*arcissistic *A*ssociation

for the

*A*dvancement

of *C*apitalistic *P*eople

1 Hip Hop the New NAACP

N = Narcissistic

Within the span of thirty days during the fall of 2009, three shocking events caused the nation to sit up and ask, "What's wrong with our youth?" On September 29th, 16 year old Chicago honor student Derrion Alberts was walking home from school and found himself in the midst of a teenage gang war. Footage from a cell phone camera captured Darien being hit in the head with a wooden plank, and then senselessly beat to death.

Stealing the headlines less than two weeks later on October 12th, five Florida teens doused a 15 year old boy with rubbing alcohol and set him on fire, then watched him burn while they laughed. The boy was punished with 2nd and 3rd degree burns over 65% of his body all because he informed police that one of the teens attempted to steal his father's bicycle from the family's front porch. Just over a week later on October 23rd, the camera lens was forced to pan left as a 15 year old Richman, California girl was raped and beaten for over two hours outside of a school dance. Police say as many as 20 teens watched or participated in the brutal attack.

The news network CNN attempted to help the nation understand what we were witnessing in these teenaged acts of immorality. They consulted their go-to education contributor Steve Perry who had this to say:

> Our children are stooping to a level of depravity that we have never seen. Our children have lost their way, in a way in which we should have never expected. Things are really bad; if you haven't visited your schools lately you should because what's coming down the pike should frighten you. It should frighten you. Children are not connected in the way in which we need them to be. This should not

be able to happen anywhere on earth.[1]

He is right, to a degree. But Mr. Perry believes that we should have never expected this. In the pages that follow I hope to show exactly why we should have expected this and what we can do to save ourselves from expecting even worse.

Concerning the above tragedies, CNN also consulted Dr. Deepak Chopra who labeled this generation "emotionally retarded," explaining that today's youth are "spiritually ungrounded" because they "have no faith." Since disconnectedness and being spiritually ungrounded are issues of culture, family and faith, we will examine these three and how they play out in the urban context. Once we are done, Hip Hop generation 1 (born in the early 1960's to mid 80's) will have the challenging responsibility of reaching back to their elders in order to grasp and then give something moral to their children – Hip Hop generation 2 (born from the mid 80's to the new millennium). Also, the remnants of the Civil Rights generation will have the frightening privilege of getting back into the life of the inner-city to appoint their successor, impart their wisdom and allocate their wealth as they collectively write their will.

If we fail at this task, future generations will judge us as they piece back together the puzzling picture of our broken world. They will study us, using the fragmented images and sound bites left behind, buried in our technological time capsules – our hard-drives and IPods and wherever else the evidence is stored. If, however, we could put those pieces together now; if we could connect the dots and decipher the matrix in our own lifetime - we would shudder at the portrait we are painting and erase our erratic etchings before the disaster-piece is complete.

The choice is simple; either we will continue on our present crash course, waiting to collide with whatever is left for a culture that has outrun family and faith; or we can go back to discover where we got off track and choose to take a new course. In order to paint an accurate picture this book will comb through popular music, movies and media, while dancing back and forth between the present and the past, to better understand how we got here and help decide how we want to move forward. What happens after we appraise the portrait will be up to each individual reader, and up to us all.

Stalled between two movements

Among the many displays of the 2008 Summer Olympics, there were three jaw dropping moments that will help to illustrate the issue at hand. In those Olympic Games the issue at hand was literally an issue at hand-off. In the 4x100 meter relay the USA men's team was favored to win. However, everyone was left stunned when the baton dropped to the ground as it was meant to pass between the 3rd and 4th leg of the race, ending their run. Coincidently, all four men running the relay for the U.S. happened to be blessed with brown-baked-clay for skin. As an American, as an African American, as an African American man – watching this was painful to the 3rd degree. Moments later, in a devastating display of déjà vu, the USA woman's team, running the same race, all of whom just so happen to be of the same race, dropped the baton at the exact same turn of the event. This was unbelievably demoralizing.

Those of us who watched instantly thought of all the factors that make the Olympics such a big deal. We recognized that based on qualifying events there were no better athletes the USA could have put on the track for that race, on that day. We considered all of the hard work these athletes had gone through to get to that point. We thought forward and accepted the reality that it would be four more years before anything close to a rematch or redemption could occur. Even more devastating, in four years, some of these runners would no longer be competing to attempt that redemptive run. These are all of the factors that make winning or losing at the Olympics such a monumental ordeal – and both teams – the men and the women, at the same spot, dropped the baton!

The third memorable moment that will be helpful for our social study is attached to the above event, yet is worthy of being an event all its own. As the baton fell to the ground between the frantically clasping clutches of Torri Edwards and Lauryn Williams, those of us watching felt our souls sink as we gave in to the gravity of the agony of defeat. Meanwhile, Lauryn Williams had decided that this was not the way she wanted her Olympic run to end. Rather than turning to point fingers at the other runner in the mishandled handoff, she turned instead to retrace her steps, chased down the renegade rod, retrieved it, and got back on track to run her leg of the race to the finish. None of us watching had even thought of such a reaction to such a disaster. All we could say was, "You Go Girl!"

Now, think of the state of urban America and where we are in the "race." If only this same course of action to be taken in the current inter-generational baton-blunder. Rather than seeking to place blame across generational lines, if we summon the courage, like Lauryn Williams, to retrace our steps, find what was lost, get back on track and finish the race, this would be bliss. But before anything like this can happen we must first identify the dropped baton, then realize what the response to this mishap has been by Runner #2 and ask whether or not it is possible to chase down and recover the wandering wand and complete our race.

Identifying the First Runner

It is generally accepted that the time it takes to produce a generation is 30 to 35 years. Therefore, Booker T. Washington and W. E. B. Du Bois were part of one generation. Roy Wilkins was part of another. Martin Luther King and Malcolm X were part of another. But a generation can also be identified by the shared attitudes and interests that mark a group of people during a specific time in history. Therefore, we will refer to all of those whose main focus in life centered on the civil rights of blacks in America collectively, as the Civil Rights generation. That would cover the entire Movement, spanning the 100 years from the end of slavery to the 1960's when something like a baton was dropped. If we can successfully acknowledge the Civil Rights Movement as one generation, sharing the same life focus, then we must ask, who is the generation that followed, and what are the shared attitudes and interests that unite them; what is the next movement? This answer will take some unpacking.

The Civil Rights Movement as the first runner overcame many hurdles: voting rights, segregation, Jim Crow laws, racial discrimination undergirded by open and often lethal brutality. Within this Movement, as movements go, there was disagreement about how to best advance the cause of the people. For instance, Roy Wilkins of the northern based National Association for the Advancement of Colored People (NAACP) had no small disagreement with Martin Luther King Jr. about the best methods to effect lasting change. As history would have it, backlash from the Montgomery, Alabama bus boycott resulted in the State of Alabama attempting to ban the NAACP from operating within its borders during the late 1950's. This worked for several years until the ruling was overturned by the Supreme Court.

During those years however, the NAACP lost its leading role in the Civil Rights Movement. Stepping in to lead the way was Martin Luther King, organizing through the Southern Christian Leadership Conference (SCLC), another civil rights organization. These two organizations had different means for fighting the same foe. One (the NAACP) focused on law-suits and laws in general to change the world for minorities. The other (the movement led by King) focused on motivating the masses into massive acts of civil disobedience in order to bring about social change.

Over time, the combined efforts of these two organizations may have worked wonders if it were not for the future, foreboding date of April 4, 1968; the day of America's one man holocaust. Seldom has it happened in the history of the world that the killing of one man could symbolize the death of so many others as in the case of Dr. King. Since his death, the NAACP has continued to do its share of jabbing at the jaw of an unjust legal system, hoping to set up and swing a knock-out blow for justice. But while the legislative approach for the advancement of colored people has managed to move along, the other side of the coin, the mass movement, was largely laid to rest with Dr. King.

Leadership, unity & the dropped baton

At the news of King's assassination it was as if the people came together to rally one last time in a destructive wave of riots that rocked the United States. But after that, it would be years before the people would strongly rally again. The voice of the NAACP could still be heard, hollering for a fair hearing from time to time. But the solo success of the NAACP without the mass mobilization of the SCLC had a strange effect on those who lived on in the nightmare world which warred against King's dream. The effect was both negative and positive; a bit of hopelessness, and yet somehow, this led to hope. Here's why:

The NAACP was sort of like Batman – it was reactionary. Something somewhere had to go wrong in order for the organization to respond to the distress signal and spring into action. They worked steadily behind the scenes, but were mostly only visible "after the fact." In July of 2009, at the opening ceremony for the NAACP's 100th anniversary, Benjamin

Todd Jealous, the organization's youngest president to date at age 36, argued that the NAACP was still needed; even though America might seem to have moved past racial issues with the election of the first black President of the United States, Barack Obama. In making his case, Jealous highlighted the reactionary nature of the organization when he said:

> On the one hand, we see the image of a black man getting off Air Force One. On the other hand, we see photos of [black] kids getting turned away from a swimming pool....We can't be post-racial until we are post-racism, and until we get there, [the NAACP] will be *on the watch.*[1]

Thankfully, they have always been "on the watch." However, their results could potentially be viewed as case specific. In other words, a legal victory for one minority might or might not apply to the next individual, and we would only find out on a case by case basis.

You might think that someone growing up with only this kind of support in their corner would be totally discouraged. And maybe so, at first. But over time, consider how this loneliness may have lightened the load for those raised in the 70's, too young to remember the murders, marches, sit-ins, speeches, rallies and riots of the Movement. If I grow up in a poor community, with social injustice, racial inequality and things of that sort; and yet the only organized challenge to these conditions comes from an organization that fights battles one at a time, focusing on a particular individual whose rights were violated, but not yet mine; AND no one really stands to combine all of the suffering I see, tying it to some common root cause – how might this affect me?

As my worldview develops, I might begin to assume that the problems facing me are mine alone, and the solution I need to seek will be mine alone. In addition, the problems facing my neighbors are theirs alone, and the solution they find will be theirs alone. There is no "us," there is only "me!" How frightening, and yet, how freeing. As Michael Eric Dyson points out, "It is much harder to think of advancing a nation, and much easier to advance myself."[2]

But, if there is no "people" then there is no longer a need for a leader. Inner-city youth will tell you today, "I don't want to be a leader. I'm just trying to be a strong individual." This is in effect the "dropped baton." What was lost when Dr. King was slain, and others like him failed to rise, was a leader who could rally us all around the issues that plague us all, black and white, rich and poor.

Now, if we are identifying the baton as 'leadership for a unified movement' and Martin Luther King symbolized this for the peak of the Civil Rights Movement, then it must be pointed out that the baton was not dropped but knocked out of the hand of the first runner. It is also true that the baton was only loosely held in the first place, since everyone was not in love with King's theology or methodology. Regardless, we must ask why neither the first nor second runner immediately chased after the stole-away-staff in order to pick it up and continue the race?

One obvious answer is the intimidation factor. King had accepted that the life of the Movement might mean his own death. He had embraced this reality long before the failure of his successful assassination. His followers would make it to the Promised Land even if, as he warned them, "I may not get there with you." But for the next outspoken leader to follow in his steps, that person might as well be saying, "Kill me too!" Dyson sees that, "King dealt with his death much better than we do. He was ready for it, we were not. He used it to propel him and his people into thoughtful action, we used it as an excuse to return to resting and rioting."[2] Having sniped and snipped this one substantial strand in the tapestry, the cultural quilt of the Civil

Rights Movement began to unravel. In turn, Runner # 1 could only turn and watch as their polemic pole, dropped and rolled away.

Runner #2

We now turn to those seeds which began to bud during the Civil Rights era. Raised in the 60s and 70s, were the children of the Movement. These youth were old enough and the struggle was still fresh enough and the hand-off still near enough to anticipate the transfer of the baton from the first runner. Some of these young people witnessed the desegregation of schools, the march on the Mall in Washington D.C. and knew that it would soon be their turn to run.

Before the baton would be passed there were several valiant strides made by our first runner in order to pick up the pace in the race "race." Even before the death of Dr. King, attempts were being made to reshape the bronze branch of leadership in order to successfully submit the scepter to the next runner. A number of urban social and political organizations had arisen in the years leading up to King's assassination. Some were more organized than others. Some were little more than (and others nothing but) glorified street gangs. One of the most organized groups was the Black Panthers of the 60s and 70s. Along with Malcolm X's writings, Bobby Seale and Huey Newton's Black Panther Party serve as testimony that not everyone was on board with King's non-violent negotiations.

The Black Panthers called for a revolution in which oppressed minorities should take up arms in self-defense to what they saw as institutionalized police brutality. They called for the end of the oppression for all groups being pinned down by America's capitalistic system. This led the Panthers to link with other "organizations" such as the Puerto Rican Young

Lords, a street gang turned political organization. Not all gangs would make this revolution evolution. In fact, some would actually devolve. The Crips street gang is possibly an example of this. Partially beginning with the hopes of providing protection from Los Angeles gangs for neighborhood boys, the Crips quickly succumbed to the perilous pleasures of gang culture. But they were not alone.

Fueled only by the dizzying fumes of despair concerning the American dream, plenty scores of professionally scorned and poverty scarred blacks either turned to or turned into quick-fix-fiends or get-rich-quick-schemes to "get by" or "get over". In other ethnic groups, the criminally minded had managed to graduate from gang activity to "organized crime," but the lack of a certain level of organization, for the most part, kept black criminal activity from earning that "distinguished" designation. None the less, "Gangta," "Pimp," "Hustla," or "Mack" (and sometimes even "Preacha") was an honorable enough title to do a little organizing still. Ambitious individuals sought to rise through the ranks in these "professions." Others were simply looking for a place to belong, and for them a street gang would do just fine.

✳ The presence of street gangs always reminds us that some unfortunate souls somewhere have been left to feel as though there were no other options. This was the case in the years following Dr. King's death.[3] Suffering from a post-pardoned-botched-baton-passing syndrome of sorts, America's urban areas hemorrhaged out miniature movements in gang-sized bites as Runner #2 tried to stride without a proper handoff. But in 1973, this second runner caught its second wind when the unexpected phenomenon of Hip Hop sprouted like Jack's beanstalk from the discarded beans of inner-city living.

Uprooted from Jamaica and planted in the Bronx NY, DJ Kool Herc (short for Hercules) brought with him the memories of portable block parties from back home. He sought to re-create those experiences with a mobile sound system that became the core element in a new culture. As Herc's sound system made its way around to different neighborhoods, people came out to celebrate "good times." Many in the Bronx, who had been displaced by the building of the Cross Bronx Expressway, were in desperate need of a social solution or maybe a social distraction or social interaction since society had overlooked them. As history would have it, these were the conditions and this was the birthplace of Runner #2 – the Hip Hop generation.

And They're Off

Some commentators claim that gang activity in New York City ceased over night when Hip Hop came on the scene. That may be too strong of a statement. The transition from bustin' heads to bustin' moves was a much more organic one. Still, the connection was undeniable. As the 1970's version of *Gangs of New York* died down, something was needed to fill the gap produced by the violence vacuum in the absence of gang wars. Word of Kool Herc's mobile merrymaking machine was getting around. A series of cultural and technological innovations was leading up to the groundbreaking arrival of a newly conceived culture.

The most important of these innovations was DJ Grand Master Flash's insightful realization that party goers, dancers in particular, seemed to routinely wait for a certain part of a record to play. This part of the record became known as the "break," usually a percussion solo with very little else accompanying. Dancers reserved their best moves for this part of the song. Flash sought to extend this "break" section by seamlessly spinning two copies of the same song's break back to back on two separate turntables. The results were abundantly successful. With this innovation, the right DJ with the right sound-system and the right records, with the right showmanship could literally rock a party all night. As it would turn out, this "break" was not just good for showcasing a DJ's ability to mix records, or for dancers to dance, it was also perfect for highlighting another facet of the emerging culture – rapping.

Rap existed before the extending of the "break beat" but became more popular as DJs used rap to rally and excite the crowd during their long sets. It was only a matter of time before others who specialized in rapping were invited on deck to "rock the mic" alongside the DJ. The party was taking on a whole new life of its own. The significance of these new cultural moves was sensed by some, yet many of these early Hip Hoppers had no idea they were taking the beginning steps of a new movement. One young man however, Afrika Bambatta, saw the emerging movement and sensed the potential power; he knew that someone had to try to codify the culture.

Bambatta had served as warlord for the Bronx street gang, the Black Spades. As the gang scene calmed down and members got older, Bambatta moved into DJing and rapping and sought to lay out a vision and mission that would serve as skeletal structure for this flesh and blood organism forming in the womb of the inner-city. To do this, he organized what he called the Zulu Nation. Using the popularity from his days as a warlord, Bam did not have to try very hard to win allegiance when he began to push this strategy for a strong union within Hip Hop. While many did not become "Zulus" in the Bambattan sense, still many others did. Looking at the charter laid out by Bambatta for his organization is instructive. He aimed to move pass the points of neighborhood protection and pride and make an attempt at progress; a progress that would not or could not wait until the NAACP prevailed; progress that would serve him and his peers in the meantime.

Abraham Maslow's "hierarchy of needs" suggests that there are certain, basic needs that must be met, in ascending order, if someone is going to thrive after managing to stay alive in this world.[4] (Figure 1.1.) The most basic of these needs are air, food and water. After these are secured, the next level is security itself - shelter and safety from the natural elements (cold, heat, rain and wind) and enemies (such as natural predators). In the 70's, these inner-city youth could not see themselves moving up to the higher levels of "need" until the issue of safety was settled.

It is to the credit of the Bronx gangs who eventually realized that the lack of safety with which they lived was largely due to their lifestyle of warring against one another. Eventually, a truce was arranged, allowing them to experience the little known euphoria of peace. We are not in complete agreement with Maslow's pecking order (we will say more about this in chapters 3 and 5), but one thing is for sure, once a degree of safety was secured, these urban youth began to move up life's ladder, or at least, up Maslow's hierarchy.

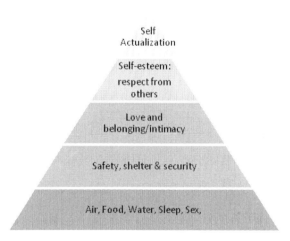

Figure 1.1

Toward the higher level of the hierarchy is what Maslow called "self-actualization." This has to do with making your mark on the world; seizing a sense of significance for the part that you play in the whole of earth's history. Of the DJs, Breakers, Rappers and Graffiti artists (the four original elements of Hip

Hop), Graffiti artists were among the first to reach for individual actualization, tagging their names on walls and trains, venturing out of their gangs "safe" territory in order to claim their share of "ghetto celebrity." But the fight for canvas space only proved that a larger platform would be needed for the leaders of this new movement. Breakers too, saw their share of the glory, but the spotlight had to shift from the floor to the stage.

Why Rappers Took the Lead

It would not be long before this budding culture would catch the eyes of the media and then industry persons seeking to expose, and or exploit it, record and recoup from it. Two notable moments occurred that carved out the lane in which this generation would run. In 1978 an independent record label would take three unsuspecting inner-city youth, along with a few "borrowed" lyrics and create the studio success *Rapper's Delight*. At an astounding fifteen minutes long (long for industry heads – short for 'in da street' heads who wondered how they were going to fit Hip Hop on a record – since Hip Hop at that time was not a four minute production, but rather the process of a party), the song was an instant classic.

But it was also an instant challenge. With commercial success in the air, a critical decision had to be made. Was Hip Hop going to be about "We the people" or "Me the person?" If men like Afrika Bambatta had their way, we suspect it would have been about the people. But once rap was seen as the cultural cash cow of ghetto, it became hard to distinguish "Hip Hop the culture," from "rap the commodity." As you read further, you will be challenged to separate the soul of "the people" from the sale of "the product."

The second significant moment has to do with another shocker which, once again, came from the rap element of the culture. In 1982 Grand Master Flash and the Furious Five reluctantly recorded *The Message* and the song actually had a message! It painted a vivid picture of what was happening on the street level of urban society. The beat was slow and contemplative; not the kind of thing you'd expect to rock a party with, and Hip Hop at that time was just that – a party. How was this going to work? And yet it did. Why did this work? "Why" is a much better question as far as we are concerned.

Remember where we are at this point in history; seven years after the assassination of Dr. King and we have a new culture on the rise. This new culture was populated by the children of the Civil Rights Movement which had lost its collective voice when King's microphone went permanently dead. Now, a decade later, after miniscule movement, the children of the Movement are finally getting back on the microphone, not just with "A Hip Hop the Hippie the Hippie to the Hip Hip Hop and you don't stop" but with a Message! How could this *not* work?

The underdog was getting back in the race and the world cheered them on. This was society, human nature, the soul for that matter, at its best; doing what it most naturally does. Like a rushing river that meets a wall which has formed against it, twists, turns, surges and pours into any opening it finds or else it creates one; these urbanites were not to be denied an expression of their ethos and pathos. And it came, 'Don't push us cuz we're close to the edge/ just tryin not to lose our heads...a   ha   ha   ha   ha.'*

---

* See *The Message* by Grand Master Flash and the Furious Five

Getting the Big Picture

1. Narcissistic means "extremely self centered." What events does the author see as leading to narcissism in the Hip Hop generation?

2. Do you see Hip Hop primarily as a culture or a category of music?

3. If Hip Hop can be seen as the "next movement" after the Civil Rights movement, what would you say is the shared interest of the Hip Hop movement?

2 Me, the Music & the Message

A = Association

Can you recall the first rap you ever heard? I was not consciously aware of the beginning stages of Hip Hop but to this day I can still remember my first encounter. It was not a rap song; however it was linked to one. I was about 8 years old. I jumped in the car with my two sisters as my father drove us to school in his light blue station-wagon with the brown wanna-be-wood paneling on the side. As we pulled up to the light in our South Philly neighborhood, my father turned on the radio. I heard the fading chorus as a song ended...something about 'Roxanne, Roxanne I wanna be your....'

But before I could catch all of the words, the disc jock interrupted, singing/saying, "If I keep hearing Roxanne so much/ I think my ears are gonna need a crutch!" I had never heard a rap song before. But I knew instantly that what this man on the radio just did was not normal. Okay, he's making a joke about how often this song is being played, I get that. But people don't talk in rhyme, with rhythm and style, in a way that instantly connects to urban-dwellers like me. Do they?

I dismissed this as an anomaly, but several years later I can remember turning on the radio hoping to find that clever communication station again. I listened to songs like *Candy* by Cameo and thought, "close, but that's not it." I stumbled onto Heavy D and the Boys' *Mr. Big Stuff* and knew I was on the right track. But it was not until I heard a tape of three white boys that I felt I had truly struck sonic gold. A bi-racial Black and Korean friend of mine by the name of Colen slid me a tape of the Beastie Boys' *License to Ill*. As I listened, it felt as if I were being let in on a secret that there was a new wave of art that expressed the heart of a new generation.

I was captivated by the playful authority with which these young men commanded my attention. They spoke, and I was listening – that is until my mother found the tape, heard the secret and smashed it to pieces before my young eyes. There was a message in the Beastie Boys' music, but it was the message of a new generation coming of age – "REBEL against everything that was here before you – especially parents." I must add that by this time in my life, at age ten, my father was no longer in the home. While he was present for my first harmless encounter with rap, it would have been nothing less than ideal had he been there for the following, more injurious points of contact with the culture. But we will save this topic for later.

Tripping Over Hip Hop

The next time I stumbled across rap was when I literally stumbled over a rap tape. Walking back from the laundromat with my mother and sister I spotted a 90 minute rainbow colored tape on the ground beneath my feet. To my surprise the tape was loaded with two of mid 80's rap's biggest names: Big Daddy Kane and the rap duo E.P.M.D. There was no turning back from that point. I became a lover of words, rhymed words, rhythm, and hard-core street beats. It was this art, and my appreciation of it, that lifted me and made me feel for the first time uncommon. Art is funny that way. When we look at an artistic work, a painting for instance, we raise its value with our esteem. And somehow, in return it raises us also. It lifts our soul, connecting us with what the Greeks called the "noumenon" - the universal ideal of Truth, Beauty, or Goodness.

At this point, I raise a word of caution to the pre-Hip Hop generation and even to Hip Hop generation 1 who struggle to appreciate the contributions of Hip Hop generation 2. Be careful not to stifle or stress the soul of a younger individual in cases where you do not find beauty in the things in which they find beauty. It is the duty of each soul, the privilege of any culture and the challenge of every generation to strive to come as close as possible to the ideals of Truth, Beauty and Goodness. And people of faith will agree that there is only One who can judge how far or how close any of us have come to it. In areas where this One has spoken, we are free to echo. Where this One is silent, our opinions should not speak louder than that silence.

A Brief History

Many others have sought to chronicle the evolution of Hip Hop, but what follows in this chapter will be a highlight reel of the turning points in Hip Hop history that deal specifically with the sociological and psychological development of the culture. If you are teaching this to your youth or learning it for the first time yourself, it might be helpful to have access to Youtube.com as a resource to research some of the names and titles cited on our short journey through Hip Hop history.

Hip Hop's recorded life has grown through many stages since its inception and it is still growing today, though some challenge the direction of this growth. Some stages have definite beginning points but hardly any has an end point because even though new stages rise, rappers still draw on the strength of previous stages and some even choose to remain exclusively on one of the prior platforms. Hip Hop began harmlessly enough in what we will call the Party stage around 1975. Slick Rick and Doug E. Fresh's *The Show*, still stands as a classic from this stage. When the opportunity to experience the spotlight and celebrity presented itself, Hip Hop welcomed the Battle Rap stage where rappers had to prove themselves worthy of holding the microphone by vanquishing rival MCs. A hallmark album that encapsulated this stage might be Big Daddy Kane's 1988 *Long Live the Kane*.

In every battle there are winners and losers. To the

winner goes the spoils and with the spoils come bragging rights; with this we enter the Braggadocio stage. Bragging sometimes has the uncanny effects of a self fulfilling prophecy. If I tell you "I'm better," or "I'm successful," or 'I'm on my way to the top," and I play the part well enough and take on that image, it won't be long before some unsuspecting soul believes me and buys into what I'm selling. This brought on the first "bling" era of the mid 80's with thick gold chains and four finger gold rings; enough to make Mr. T. look like one of the boys in the hood. Consider Special Ed's 1989 hit *I Got It Made*. He bragged of getting a brand new car every other week, having seventy-four Honda scooters, owning an island in Tahiti and having a dog with a solid gold bone, saying, "I make all the money from the rhymes I invent."

Listeners knew that this was pure wishful thinking and an exaggeration of the most extreme hyperbole, but just think if it were true in the slightest. There was also the subconscious suspicion that because he was saying "I got it made" all over the radio, he might actually sell enough records to make some of those lyrics a reality. But this was too far from reality for too many people. In fact, on the West Coast, something was brewing that would forever change the culture; a brand of Hip Hop that, at its most glorious moments in 1988 and '89 was actually called 'Reality rap,' and every notorious moment after that, known as Gangsta rap.

The rappers who popularized this expression of the culture called themselves "street reporters." Their job, they claimed, was to let the rest of the world know what really happens in the "hood," though it soon became clear that many of these "reporters" were also the very culprits providing the colorful storyboards for their editorials. NWA's *Straight Outta Compton* took America by storm and caused a hail storm of criticism, most notably a battle with political activist C. Deloris Tucker. Controversy sells and record labels scrambled to find other artists who could sell the Gangsta rap image like NWA.

While all of this was taking place on the West Coast, in the early to mid 90's the East Coast was organizing itself in a consortium of cliques, squads and crews. There seemed to be an elevated interest in the "strength in numbers" theory. It became more common to see artists from certain cliques together instead of separate; not as a group, but as a group of groups. Ultra talented MCs, dream-teams, came together to produce super-hero-ish collaborations, such as Leader's of the New School's *The Scenario*. Popular names from this stage include the Boot Camp Clique, The Def Squad and most notably, The Wu Tang Clan. Grimy, rugged and unpolished was the expression in music and fashion. This is when Timberland boots were adopted as the footwear of choice on the East Coast, even on the hottest summer day with the latest fashion.

Go West Young Man

Across the country in California, Dr. Dre's *The Chronic* album was tipping the scale radio wise, causing airwave support to favor the flavor of the melodic, hypnotic, Dr. Dre and Snoop Dogg, Long Beach sound. One reason for this lop-sidedness in airplay was that East Coast rap was known for being heavily focused on 'mastering the mic;' the art of MCing. Because of this, lyrics often outshined the accompanying musical production which tended to be sample driven and methodical. This was good for providing a platform and allowing listeners to focus on what mattered most to the artist – his lyrics. The samples of East Coast rap did more than just leave room for lyrics to shine. They also helped to celebrate and connect youth to their cultural, musical past, sampling the sounds of James Brown and others. Sampling allowed inner-city youth to connect with other cultures as well. In the early 90's, it was not uncommon to hear rap songs where the main sample was a piano or violin loop from a classical recording.

But cities to the west were expanding the sound, breaking free from music of the past. Lyrics now synchronized and sympathized with synthesized notes from keyboards which breathed a melodious air of freedom into the music: freedom from stiff, seemingly, stifling samples; freedom from the pre-recorded, pre-packaged past; and most excitingly, individuality and freedom from the entity known as the East Coast. .

Late night radio, on the other hand, was becoming increasingly friendlier to the underground East Coast sound. More radio shows began to create formats for "underground" rap, even on the West Coast where it was assumed that East Coast rap would not be well received. It was not just the music, but the subject matter differed greatly as well. In the east, rappers focused on skills, lyricism, being deep and scientific. Rappers would rap about the mic itself as if it were their personal creation, slave, friend, weapon, partner, nemesis, surgical tool, or mistress. On the West Coast, rap was more laid back, it was about one's life or life-style, be it chillin' or 'mobbin' and gang-banging. Often it lacked the technical elements of MCing that won respect on the East Coast, with the exceptions of artists such as Ahmad, the Hieroglyphics or the Tunnel Rats. That being said, for years the West Coast had one of the most recognized rap-skill celebrating Hip Hop radio shows, *The Wake Up Show* with Sway and Tech (Tek).

Gangstas and Thugs

The mid 90's also saw the rise of another stage – the thug rapper. This role was popularized by artists such as Bone Thugs & Harmony and Tupac Shakur. The thug was a bit different from the gangsta rapper. While the gangsta rapper said, "I'm just as hard and wild as the streets that raised me," the thug seemed to say in effect, "the ends justify the means." Jay Z, who reigned in Hip Hop as an MC from 1997 (after the death of Biggie Smalls and Tupac Shakur) until at least 2005, even released a song entitled *Justify My Thug*, in which this mentality is laid out in full. There is a very thin (and often crossed) line between the gangsta and the thug, but it is the difference between the "thug" saying, "I gotta do what I gotta do" and the "gangsta" saying in the words of Al Pacino's Scarface character (a celebrated figure in Hip Hop) "I do this for fun!"

In the mid 90's, rap was still not a staple in the radio format of American music, not even in the urban markets. Two things happened that forced this to change. In the summer of 1992, the soon to be crowned Queen of Hip Hop/Soul, Ms. Mary J. Blige released the *Real Love* single. This was one of the first, if not the first R&B song to use an unmistakably branded, Hip Hop break-beat as its core. If you ask a teenaged person today to name the four original elements of Hip Hop, they will undoubtedly list R&B as one of the elements. But it was not until 1992 that rap and R&B kissed and became overtime, an inseparable couple. Today it is rare to hear an R&B song without a rap verse attached. This break-beat broke tradition and helped pave the way for radio to become friendly to rap that wasn't "radio-friendly." Before this, rap music had to sound ultra commercial (think MC Hammer) in order to make it into radio rotation in a broad day-light broadcast.

The other ground breaking event in the mid 90's that opened the gates for Hip Hop in the mainstream was the advent of a dynamic duo made up of the late rapper Biggie Smalls aka The Notorious B.I.G. and producer Sean Puffy Combs aka Puff Daddy aka Diddy. In the rap category, Biggie entered in on the Thug stage, as he starts off one of his early hit singles, *Juicy*, by rubbing his success in the face of "all the people that lived above the buildings I was [selling drugs] from, that called the police on me when I was *just* trying to make some money to feed my daughter." Notice the justification.

The different stages of Hip Hop began to merge at this

point. With the successful blend of Biggie's raps and Diddy's production (a clever technique of reselling old school hit's from the 80's), Biggie, Puffy and the entire Bad Boy Entertainment entourage ushered in Hip Hop's second "Bling" era, which successfully merged elements from the Party stage, the Battle stage, the Braggadocio stage, and the Thug stage all into one collective presentation.

In the new millennium, Hip Hop left the actual stage for a time and went back to the floor, ushering in a Dance Move era, with new trends arriving weekly or monthly. Popular dances from this period include D-macking, Krumping, Wu-tanging, old school pop-locking and break-dancing, doing the Stanky-leg or the Soldja Boy, named after the artist who originated the dance, and my personal favorite (not really), Chicken Noodle Soup with a Soda on the Side.

Even with all of this, we have not yet covered all of the stages of Hip Hop to date. I am sure that students of the culture are right now wondering where I got my Hip Hop history degree from for having left out two key turning points in the timeline. I have purposely saved these two very important stages for our next discussion, during which we will develop a holistic picture of Hip Hop's journey in America. If I have rushed through your favorite stage, fear not. We will come back with needle and thread to sew all of this together. And if I have not touched on your particular brand of Hip Hop just yet, don't worry. It may be that we have saved the best for last.

So far I have only given my personal experience of Hip Hop. You may have experienced these stages in a drastically different manner and that is okay. But from this point on we are diving into the deep end of the pool. Our language will be a bit more technical and academic. The perspective will also aim to be more objective. As the reader, you must consider how the historical events of the following chapters have not only affected

Hip Hop, but how they and Hip Hop have affected you.

Getting the Bigger Picture

1. How might the term "association" apply to Hip Hop in this chapter?

2. Two important stages of Hip Hop have not yet been mentioned, can you identify which two?

3. Which stage of Hip Hop do you most identify with? (Or which stage are you most familiar with?)

3 The Ghost of Hip Hop Past

A = Advancement

$\mathcal{H}$istory has a way of repeating itself. It especially likes to make repeat appearances upon those who've missed it the first time and who, through lack of study, are mystified by its current recurrence. The old quote still holds true, "Those who don't know their past are doomed to repeat it," and Hip Hop is no exception to that rule. In 2003, I began my first year at Lancaster Bible College. I had spent 9 years traveling and performing as a Christian Hip Hop artist and public speaker, written numerous articles for online and a few print publications and spoken on the subject of faith and culture quite frequently. But it wasn't until that year, in my first English course with Mrs. Piepgrass, that I met two over-arching figures from the pages of black history - Booker T. Washington and W. E. B. Du Bois. (Blame my public school education)

As I studied the lives and literature of these two opposing leaders, I couldn't shake the feeling that I had heard their 100 year old arguments somewhere before. Not in the distant past, but that very week. But where? Have you ever heard a melody, or maybe even just a couple of notes that remind you of a song, only you can't quite catch the tune? If so, then you know how I felt. I strained to recognize the familiar music in the words of Du Bois and Washington and then suddenly, like a car jumping the curb, it hit me. Through modern day Hip Hop, the haunting harp of history was echoing pages from the hymnal of African American history. As I retell the tale of these two men, listen and see if you can hear what I heard before we return back to the future in the next chapter.

The historical context

In 1820, the Mason-Dixon Line became the dividing line between free and slave states in America. This division lasted forty-five years until America's bloody Civil War, after which, the South's black population was finally, functionally emancipated. Upon being freed, many set their eyes on one particular prize - education. Before emancipation, slaves were legally blocked from learning to read or write. In fact, "The more commercial a proposition slavery became, the more drastic were the laws enacted against education [of blacks....But with] the outbreak of the Civil War, Negro slaves began to be educated in fairly large numbers" as they escaped to the North.[1]

While blacks served in the Union forces, schools began springing up like wells to quench their thirst for knowledge. Once the war ended education was even more hotly pursued by blacks since education was seen as essential in order for a person to understand his economic and political interests. This became a major issue over the next thirty years. America engaged in a battle of ideas concerning Reconstruction of the war-torn country and how to solve "the Negro problem." The main question was, how much, if at all, should blacks be helped onto their feet by the government and how much should they be left to work their way up on their own, which was seen as the "American way."

As freed men began to work and vote, labor unions and politicians saw that blacks could help to sway the political direction of the country in their favor. Labor unions favored a style of government that was very close to, if not exactly like socialism (communism), which would raise the individual worker to an equal status with employers, who were seen as unfair and even inhumane to workers. Politicians favored capitalism and feared communism. In those days Republicans, more than Democrats, were sympathetic to the plight of blacks and looked to play a role in their social development. As African American's organized they found they would have to choose sides. Some blacks accepted that over a long period of time, progress would come as they worked hard and gradually earned the respect of whites; on the other side, stood blacks who sought immediate change through social and political action.

The South was looked at as a proving ground for African Americans since most of the country's blacks were still southerners at this time. They were told that if they just worked like the white man works then northern markets would open up for them and that "the negroes of this country could press their demand for equality of treatment as laborers with much better [chances] of success than...[through] mistaken political legislation."[2] This was said partially from belief, but also from a southern, white fear that a powerful black political movement could affect a vote where former slaves would end up with the land of their former masters. In 1884, after moving north to New York, African American journalist T. Thomas Fortune wrote:

> When the government freed the slaves and gave the vote, it added four million men... to the laboring masses....It also added four millions of souls to what have been termed...the dangerous classes' – meaning...the vast army of men and women who...threaten to take by force from society that which society prevents them from making honestly.[3]

Fearing this, any workers who organized with labor unions or complained about the system; any African American who moved toward political activism; all who looked at capitalism with a suspect eye were labeled as "disaffected," troublesome and out to use the government to impose African American dominance on society. After years of this kind of propaganda from southern whites, sometimes hidden behind vicious lies about black men hunting and raping white women, whites in the North reacted out of fear and practically gave their blessing to the South to deal with this dark threat. As portrayed in the 1915 film *The Birth of a Nation*, disfranchisement, intimidation, discrimination, brutality and lynching blacks became common and acceptable in the South.

Even African Americans themselves begin to justify these acts and looked to separate themselves from the type of black person these things could happen to. Some blacks criticized those in the past who had taken the government's aid saying, "The men of the emancipation generation had depended on others for their needs rather than participating in self-help."[4] "Self-help" was the American creed. This was ironic since much of America's rich success with capitalism was based on the forced or cheap labor of others and not "self." Rather than voicing this or taking political action, it was safer for southern blacks to play by the capitalistic rules that America seemed to value. Into this volatile context came W.E.B. Du Bois and Booker T. Washington.

School Daze

W.E.B. Du Bois was born February 23rd 1868, north of the Mason-Dixon Line in Great Barrington, Massachusetts, free from the tyranny of slavery. On the other side of the divide stands Booker T. Washington. Born a slave on a plantation in Franklin County, Virginia around 1858, the exact date of his birth is unknown, which was common among slaves. He was freed along with the nation's black population in the South during the Civil War. Both men brilliant, both men distinguished and highly honored, and each is known as the first black man to receive a degree from Harvard. The difference in the types of degrees they received made all the difference in the world. The debate between Du Bois and Washington can be seen through the history of higher education in America which was undergoing drastic change, just as blacks were getting ready to enter the school house doors.

Harvard, founded in 1636, is the Nation's oldest institute of higher education. Since the time of European immigration to America, this country's educational heritage has sprang from the north-east corridor between New England and Pennsylvania.[5] Of America's three oldest institutions, Harvard and Yale are north-eastern schools and William and Mary is located to the south, in Virginia. The founding documents of all three schools set forth the aim of educating moral, social and practical ministers. The curriculum matched that aim – "Classical languages [and] grounding in the three basic philosophies of Aristotle, ethics, metaphysics and... science. The education offered was a practical one for the seventeenth and eighteenth century."[6] But the nineteenth century brought change to the world of higher learning. Harvard students were becoming less interested in studies and piety. At William and Mary, students seemed to only want a thin slice of liberal education, and almost none graduated.[7] Harvard got over this disinterest by creating two separate fields of study, one for divinity and one for mathematics and science.

These institutions flirted with lowering their admissions standards and lessoning their emphasis on Latin and Greek, the "classical languages." However, as new students became unruly, the schools returned to the classical languages in an attempt to introduce a degree of mental discipline.[8] This failed however, since the true purpose of those classic and sacred texts was mainly moral discipline and not simply mental exercise. In the 1820's these colleges were verbally attacked for their obsession with "dead languages" and for neglecting more practical subjects. Throughout the 1800's institutes of higher education struggled because of their focus on the "culture of the mind." In 1889, one of the wealthiest men in history, Andrew Carnegie criticized:

> While the college student has been learning a little about the barbarous and petty squabbles of a far-distant past, or trying to master languages which are dead, (such knowledge as seems adapted for life upon another planet than this as far as business affairs are concerned) the future captain of industry is hotly engaged in the school of experience, obtaining the very knowledge required for his future triumphs...College education as it exists is fatal to success in that domain.[9]

This pressure helped pave the way for "the university," which was designed around the idea of adding more practical, technology based subjects to the roster without abandoning classical education.

School Rivals

If you do not yet hear the Hip Hop harmony to this part of history, it is only because Du Bois and Washington have not yet joined the chorus. But here they come. With the end of slavery and the Reconstruction efforts dragging on, both the North and the South grew tired of trying to solve the Negro problem. In 1890, writer Henry M. Fields concluded, "African Americans must be unable to rise, or the past decades of equality would have created a prosperous black community. It is disappointing and discouraging to find that, with all these opportunities, they are little removed from where they were a hundred years ago."[10]

One of the most hotly debated "opportunities" for blacks was education, namely what type of education should blacks receive? Being a practical man from the South, Booker T. Washington saw that capitalism ruled the day. What mattered was measured in Yds, Acres and Mls. The accumulation of land and wealth in the family's name would help his people rise *Up From Slavery*. He therefore favored a hands-on type of schooling that would teach money earning trades to blacks. But to Du Bois, what mattered most were the letters that appear behind one's own name: BS, MS, PH.D., so long as the degrees were actually earned and not merely conferred. The key was not the economy, but education. He therefore favored a higher level of learning for his people.

Washington's message to his people, and to whites, was that blacks were willing to work while waiting for change. Voting, civil rights, equality, etc. all of that would come eventually if blacks could prove that they too valued the capitalistic "work my way up from the bottom" approach. He seemed to settle for segregation in his Atlanta Compromise speech where he said, "When it comes to business, pure and simple, it is in the South that the Negro is given a man's chance in the commercial world....In all things that are purely social [blacks and whites] can be as separate as the fingers, yet one as the hand in all things essential to mutual progress."

One critic summed up his speech as saying to southern whites, "Only by lessoning antagonism against the Negro can you properly use him in getting rich."[11] Washington himself went to a technical school and after teaching for a while, made his life's work Tuskegee University, a trade school for colored men and women. Focusing on this and ignoring all other grievances, he saw "as the best way to advance the status of Negroes in American society."[12]

Du Bois however, was thinking larger than the Negro in America, he was thinking about *The Souls of Black Folk* in the broader scope of the universe. He saw Washington's "work and wait" policy as settling for less than full rights and manhood. Du Bois' method was "educate and agitate." He wrote that, "In the history of nearly all other races and peoples, the doctrine preached at such crises [as this] has been that mainly self-respect is worth more than lands and houses and that a people who voluntarily surrender such respect or cease striving for it, are not worth civilizing."[13]

Du Bois co-founded the NAACP in 1909. He studied and wrote on every aspect of the black experience in America, especially the psychological torment of being both African and American, what he called "double consciousness." Du Bois saw that what really made men and women free was the life of the mind and not just the daily grind. When it came to education he valued the classical approach and believed the goal should be to "carry a child as far as possible in the accumulated wisdom of the world....and then when economic or physical reasons demand that this education must stop, vocational training to prepare for life work should follow."[14]   But ideally education would never stop. Putting forth a creed for youth, Du Bois called for education, "adequate, expertly taught, and continuing through the elementary grades, through high school ...beyond the school years in the form of adult education."[15]   Without this, even though his people might rise financially, they would still be oppressed politically and spiritually.

But Du Bois saw a golden opportunity. He perceived that the conditions of the South – the lynching, the lack of schools, and disfranchisement, had finally made blacks ready for change. A major sign of this was that in the early 1900's blacks were moving to the North in record numbers; skilled, intelligent and educated blacks that the South could not afford to lose. But he observed that "the level of intelligence and efficiency in these newcomers is almost inevitably below that of the Negro already established in the North." He had a solution, however. There were three groups of people who had already tried to solve the Negro problem – farmers, manufacturers, and labor unions. Instead of investing in technical schools that merely teach trades, why not invest in a fourth group – the northern Negro.[16]

Du Bois called for "the education of a talented tenth of the [black] population, to lead the American Negro into a higher civilization, rather than having to accept white leadership which could not always be trusted to guide this group into *self realization* and to its highest cultural possibility."[17] It has been estimated that ninety percent of the nations black population lived in the South at this time and by Du Bois' own count the South contained 9,000,000 blacks while only 1,725,141 black folk resided in the North.[18, 19,] His "talented tenth" theory called for white philanthropists to invest in northern black intellectuals to come to the rescue of the southern Negro; not simply because they were southerners but because they had been socialized in the region where America's capitalistic clutches had clamped down on the souls of his people.

In making his case, Du Bois criticized what he called the "General backwardness of the southern states in education."[20] Even when it came to religious education he noted that though there was plenty of fervor and faith in the South, "Theology and religious philosophy are...a long way behind the North."[21] He charged southern black schools like Hampton with the crime of burying genius and talent and not sifting to find the brightest African Americans in order to send them on to higher education. No artists, no writers were being produced in the technical schools of the South and these black schools seemed to operate on the "assumption that every Negro must be trained to farm...or be a servant." For these reason, Du Bois believed that such schools did not belong to black people, "but to the white South and reactionary North."[22]

But Booker T. Washington was not silent in criticizing those who received the type of higher education Du Bois thought so highly of. As "learned" students came also to his "hands-on" school, Washington smirked:

It was interesting to note how many big books some of them had studied, and how many high-sounding subjects some of them claimed to have mastered. The bigger the book and the longer the name of the subject, the prouder they felt of their accomplishment. Some had studied Latin, and one or two Greek. This they thought entitled them to special distinction.[23]

He teased that they had remembered "long and complicated rules in grammar and mathematics but had little knowledge of applying these rules to everyday life." He also felt that many only sought higher learning because they hoped to be teachers so they would not have to work with their hands.

Washington's assessment played right into the general thinking of the time. Universities were broadening their curriculum to include more technologies and science, lifting them to the status of "professional fields" which used to only include philosophy and theology, then medicine and law. On top of this, many did not believe blacks would benefit from old school classical education. Du Bois almost gave in, sadly confessing that the black student of higher education was:

Pushed toward an elaborate preparation that over-fitted him for his lowly tasks. The would-be black savant was confronted by the paradox that the knowledge his people needed was a twice-told tale to his white neighbors, while the knowledge which would teach the white world was Greek to his own flesh and blood.[24]

In other words, the higher education that white America had grown tired and bored with, those ancient, metaphysical paths to morality, comprised the very education that his own people so desperately needed.

Du Bois wrote that while whites were not better than any other ethnicity throughout the history of the world, still, just like Rome, and Greece before that, "Europe and the western world, [had] learned from and built on other great cultures of the past

[and] have gone forward to greater and more splendid human triumph," having built their foundation on the science and religion of "Nefertari, Mohammad, Ramses, and Askia, Confucius, Buddha, and Jesus Christ."[25] Du Bois warned the western world not to forget those great moral and social instructors.

Because Du Bois was so adamant about the mental and moral education of the soul of his people, he was shut out of the new university scheme. Meanwhile, by co-signing the capitalistic agenda, Washington's school received continued acceptance and funding. It was thought that Washington's technical schools would instantly help blacks learn the skills needed to add to the economy. But if whites had funded Du Bois ideas, more thinkers might only result in more ideas. And for many whites in those days, 'thinker' was too high and mighty a title for blacks; 'worker' was high enough. This hateful and narrow minded view was put forth by Senator Benjamin Tillman of South Carolina after President Theodore Roosevelt had dinner with Booker T. Washington in 1901. Tillman's hateful lips parted to pronounce, "The action of President Roosevelt in entertaining that nigger will necessitate our killing a thousand niggers in the South before they learn their place again."[26] For him, Blacks could not exist on the same level; they were beneath whites in the hierarchy.

Realization vs. Actualization

Du Bois often used the terms "self-conscious" and "self realization" as a goal for the souls of black folk. This sounds similar to Maslow's goal of "self actualization," (discussed in chapter one) but there is a major difference between the two. Maslow's hierarchy climaxes with "self actualization" which is something that must be achieved, not conceived; worked for, not worked out. We must craw and claw our way to the top, scraping and scrapping, all the while hoping to make it. Washington approached this hierarchy in the "American way" where no one naturally starts out at the higher end. He focused on the lower levels; 'how are we going to eat and secure shelter and be safe from the natural elements and enemies?' In other words, what position do we have to fold ourselves into in order to survive?

Du Bois' response was simple, 'What's the use of surviving if we're going to have to live like slaves, marketing ourselves as merchandise, never marching as men?' Du Bois seemed to be saying the very opposite of Maslow. We do not start from the bottom and hope to make it to the top; rather, through the "realization" that we are already at the top, the bottom levels now become the common right of us all.

Bottom's Up

Think of how Maslow's bottom-up approach to life has impacted our world. If life is first and foremost about securing one's own access to food, water and air, then a person is pretty much justified in doing whatever they have to do in order to score those supplies. One can hardly be concerned with anything else until they do. Darwinian evolution approaches life with Maslow's bottom-up hierarchy at heart where life is reduced to "survival of the fittest." Those who are physically or mentally fit enough to secure their needs will live and make it to the top, while all the rest might just as well go hungry and die. Maslow combines with evolution to teach that this is natural. But if that were so, mothers would naturally leave infants to fend for themselves and we would not be so shocked or appalled when we hear of negligent parents.

Looking back at the horrors of the Civil War, Du Bois commented that this hierarchical approach to life had led to "dark and awful depths and not to the shining and ineffable heights of which" modern culture boasted.[27] This bottom-up approach corrupts the systems of capitalism and communism just the same. Capitalism says that, 'everyone should be free to become as wealthy as their will and skill can allow.' Communism says, 'because we are all equally valuable, everyone should work according to their ability but should only receive according to their need.' One of the main dangers of capitalism's limitless wealth approach is that we begin to value people based on how profitable they are to us and we can even begin to value profit above people. Communism sounds flattering at first, but can be a tricky subject as well because of Maslow's bottom up approach. The few who sit at the top get to decide everyone's ability to work and what everyone else's needs happen to be. Somehow, those at the top always end up "needing" and getting more.

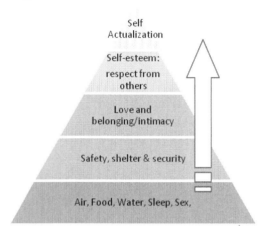

Both communism and capitalism have led to only a few making it to the top, ending up with very much, while very many remain at the bottom and end up with very little. How is this possible? It's simple; because in actuality, we are not simply evolved animals with instinct. We are human beings with animated intellect. But if we are led to follow and swallow the theory of evolution and live up to Maslow's hierarchy, then our animated intellect will begin to imagine ways to use and exploit our fellow human beings. Why? Because according to Maslow, life is fundamentally about food, and animals use whatever natural tools they have to secure their sustenance. Why shouldn't we use our minds to motivate, move or manipulate others who may be competing for the same food and water as ourselves? The benefits could be enormous. It is the classic case of 'loving things and using people' instead of 'using things and loving people.'

These ideas come from the top of the hierarchy and then trickle down to the street level where most of us live. On the street, the phrase, "I'm just tryna to eat," has become a common colloquialism for staying alive. If a young mother needs to feed her hungry children, stripping in a club, dancing on a pole and possibly selling her body is understandable because after all (or before all) "I gotta eat." Again, if we start from the bottom and have to work our way up, a young man may feel justified in saying, "I'm hungry, So&So has food and I don't, but I'm stronger or have the tools to get what I want from him." Or maybe "I'll sell this addictive, destructive substance to her. It's her fault for being weak enough to need it. And after all (or before all), I gotta eat!"

Upside Down

Although Booker T. Washington would certainly not have approved of illegal or immoral activity in order to rise up from slavery, he seemed to accept this bottom-up reasoning where the ends justify the means, like Hip Hop's thug. Consider the difference between "actualization's" bottom-up approach and "realization's" top-down approach. In a September, 2008 radio interview with host (and Hip Hop legend) Ed Lover, rapper Jay-Z was asked how he felt about religious people admonishing him for calling himself "god" and "J-hova." He responded, "I think that if religious people read their text correctly [referring to the Bible's Genesis 1:26] we're all made in the image of God, so calling yourself 'god' is not blasphemous."[28] A more biblical understanding of the image of God is offered in chapter 13, but for now we can say that the idea of the image of God in man should, if nothing else, lead to a top-down approach.

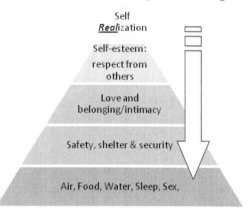

If I realize that I am created in God's image, this gives me a certain dignity and worth. Because of this, I have a right to all of the lower levels in the hierarchy, all the way down to the most basic. If this is so, then I must ask 'what are the acceptable ways for someone who reflects God's image to secure these basic needs?' And while I'm at it, how can I be mindful of others who, just like me, draw their self-worth from our common Creator, and just like me, deserve to eat, vote, buy, sell or whatever? This approach sounds strange but only because we are fed bottom-up ideals in every bit and sound-bite of American life where self has become supreme and society is secondary. People do not view one another as existing at the top, and most struggle to "get there."

Connecting the dots

What has history shown? African Americans have been valued, not so much as members of society, but as merchandise. As a race, blacks have mainly advanced when they've proven their ability to provide valuable services to their fellow white citizens, not only as laborers, but especially in the area of the arts. Race relations in America have been exponentially advanced because of talented blacks who have contributed to America's cultural and recreational life. Indeed, before Barack Obama was elected president, it was tremendously difficult for high school students (black or white) to think of a well known African American who has benefited them outside the realms of art and entertainment.

When Michael Jordan finally retired from the NBA, during his last game in Philadelphia against the 76ers, the final quarter was interrupted by the (majority white) crowd with what seemed like an eternity of applause and praise for the man who had inspired and entertained them for years. Another MJ got a similar salute. During the week following the death of Michael Jackson, it was amazing to witness the amount of coverage his life and legacy received from news stations such as CNN. *Charlie's Angels* star Farrah Fawcett had died the same day. North Korea was threatening to wipe North America off the face of the earth; Iran was wrestling with civil unrest in the streets due to a disputed presidential election; back in the United States, congress was battling with President Obama over healthcare reform, and yet, for five days, all of these stories only appeared as tag lines at the bottom of the screen. The big story was the larger than life legacy of innovator/entertainer, Michael Jackson.

During that coverage, CNN interviewed cultural critic Kevin Powell, who put in a plug for his upcoming book in which he explores how the successes of black entertainers such as Jordan and Jackson actually paved the way for whites to be able to accept and elect Barack Obama. We can add to this the fact that Obama won the presidential election largely because he appeared to be the most qualified candidate to help America out of its financial woes. Our country's mindset of a person's personal worth is rooted in their ability to add to our own comfort and wealth. Because after all (or before all) "we gotta eat."

Applying this to our discussion of North and South is not hard. Even though slavery had ended, Du Bois saw that the newly publicized theory of evolution, combined with capitalism, spelled trouble for his people. He warned that there was a time when science did not regard race, but "the attitude of science toward colored races greatly changed" in the nineteenth century. This new "science" left whites with the question:

> As to how far the earth is inhabited by nations and races essentially equal in their gifts and power of accomplishment, *or* how far the world is a hierarchy headed by the white people, with other groups graduating down by grades of color to smaller and smaller brain power, ability and character.[29]

Du Bois saw this raced based hierarchy as an "attack on the concept of God." Even though he was for educating a "talented tenth" of the black population, for him "the world of the intellect was not a social ladder from which to escape the cares of his fellow blacks down below. Instead, intellect could be the salvation of the blacks and of all the oppressed."[30]

Du Bois and Washington both received degrees from Harvard. Du Bois was the first African American to earn Harvard's PH.D., while Washington was the first African American to receive their honorary Master's degree; not for his studies at Harvard, but for the work he accomplished at his technical school in Tuskegee. Du Bois later remarked that he saw "conferred degrees" as more commercial then commemorative.[31] Nonetheless, the two degrees strike a familiar chord: northern blacks can learn, while southern blacks can be used to earn and that's just how the songs goes.

This music has now ended, or at least the older version of the song has. Before you turn the page, take a moment to see if you can identify a more modern version of this old tune. Most minds will rush to the Martin vs. Malcolm arguments of the Civil

Rights era, but there is an even more recent remix that perfectly parallels this history. In the next chapter, listen as the chimes dazzle while we time travel back to the future and attempt to name that tune.

Getting the Big Picture

1.   If it were up to you at the time, which do you believe you would have supported more - the ideas of Booker T. Washington's or W.E.B. Du Bois' for advancement of the African Americans?

2.   How do you think things might have turned out differently if more money had been invested into the ideas of Du Bois instead of Washington?

3.   Would you approach Maslow's Hierarchy from the bottom up or from the top down?

4.   If from the top down, what are some actual ways you could do this in your daily life/relationship/opportunities?

4 Bringing the Future Back

C = Capitalistic

*D*o you now hear what I heard? If you know your Hip Hop history you are probably humming along like a human harmonica, harmonizing with history's harp as it hits each nostalgic note and strikes a chord. For those who may have missed the modern musical, we will now rehearse the new millennium version of North and South. As you read, look for remnants of the Reconstruction.

In 2001, a major shift was occurring in the Hip Hop world. The entire axis of orbit was about to tip to the south with such momentum, it was as if the inner-city was being turned upside down. New York struggled to remain the hub. But Hip Hop had hit the road; Texas to St. Louis then New Orleans and finally an extended stay in Atlanta. What used to count as rap skills was now either 'old school' or worse – 'corny.' Things were being said from below the Mason-Dixon Line that hit below the belt.

In 2010, new southern rapper Waka Flocka Flame was still echoing ten year old insults at northern rappers. "Don't nobody wanna hear that god-damned dictionary rap. I don't need no lyrics to make money. The average person that they call lyrical...ain't eatin'."[1] From the turn of the new millennium, Hip Hop had a stage in the South. This new stage, however, seemed to clash with another key stage in Hip Hop which began in the mid 80's and continues to this day: the stage of Edutainment or Conscious rap.

Signs of Consciousness

In 1982, when the Hip Hop classic, *The Message* was

released, the record went platinum in less than a month. The socially conscious song took Hip Hop in a different direction than just the party. Queens, NY rapper Nas recalled, "When I heard Melle Mel send *The Message*, it changed my life. It just sounded like...some prophet."[2] Not more than five years later, the Hip Hop world would begin to hear from other messengers; rappers who sounded more like thinkers and teachers, philosophers at the podium or preachers in the pulpit. Through Hip Hop, these rappers had found the perfect classroom, full of bright-eyed (and perhaps dingily-clothed) students who lived for or in the Big Apple on the teacher's desk.

Artists who ushered in this stage include Rakim, with his cerebral lyrics and hypnotic flow, who brought his Five-percent Nation of gods and earths* lessons to his music; Public Enemy, who served as a lyrical, theatrical expression of the Nation Of Islam's more militant message; and KRS ONE with his metaphysical leanings toward meaning. These artists perfected the art of educating while entertaining and overtime, gave birth to what would come to be called "Conscious rap."

The genre is called "conscious" because the artists who represent it are said to be 'awake' or 'aware' of what individuals in the inner-city are *really* up against. Also, these artists are best described as "conscious" because they once served as the conscience of Hip Hop culture overall and provided a sense of spirituality for the masses. The conscious rapper was once revered as a sort of superhero, while the culture, like Lois Lane kept ending up in harm's way. Over the years the conscious torch has been passed along and carried by such artists as Common, Mos Def, Talib Kweli and Lupe Fiasco.

This does not include 'Positive rap' which 'Conscious rap' is sometimes confused or combined with. What we

---

* Among other beliefs discussed later in this chapter, Five-percenters believe that the black man is the original man/god.

commonly call 'positive rap' is actually not positive, but amoral – neither negative nor positive. Will Smith's rap style is often referred to as positive because of the absence of negatives. However, the absence of negativity does not automatically mean the presence of positivity, i.e. what one should do, or how one should be[have]. *

An important contribution of the Edutainment stage was the language and lifestyle it prompted. The Ancient Greeks, who pursued all knowledge concerning man and his world, coined the phrase, "Know Thyself." Conscious rappers in the early 90's coined a similar phrase, "Knowledge of Self." This charge was led by Five-percenters in New York City and provided a convenient point of contact with the culture for little known Christian rappers. The pursuit for "knowledge of self" led to young people discussing ancestry, history and especially religion, openly on inner-city streets. This was all a reflection of the music. Groups like X-Clan, Poor Righteous Teachers and The Native Tongues (made up primarily of Hip Hop's legendary innovative ensemble, A Tribe Called Quest, De La Soul, and the Jungle Brothers), emerged and helped to etch an afro-centricity into our collective consciousness. This led to people wearing medallions of Africa around their necks as a sign that they did indeed possess "knowledge of self." YZ's *Master Plan* and Intelligent Hoodlum's *Black and Proud* forcefully represent this stage.

The impact of the Edutainment stage can be seen in other fashions from those days. Watch an old re-run of the *Cosby Show* college-based spinoff *A Different World* and you will see several individuals donning locked hair, Kente cloth or some other connection to Africa as part of their attire. The show ran from 1987 to 1993, the dawn of Hip Hop's Edutainment stage,

---

* We discuss the issue of positive rap more thoroughly in the final chapter

which heavily influenced the series. These cultural trends were significant since they may have also helped to reverse another social trend which began in the 1950s after the landmark case of Brown v. The Board of Education; the trend that put *White Teachers in Diverse Classrooms*, as one book points out:

> During desegregation as blacks were bussed out of their neighborhoods to white schools, "41,600 African American teachers were demoted or dismissed...[from then on] African American college students who might have aspired to teach saw teaching...as a White woman's work.[3]

This "brought black male youth into conflicting relationships with white women teachers." This condition still exists today since "only about 7 percent of all teachers in America are African American and less than 2 percent are African American males."[4, 5] But according to the National Association of Student Financial Aid Administrators reports that "the number of education bachelor's degrees earned by minorities, was low in the 1980s, [but] rebounded in the 1990s" and saw a "9 percent growth rate [by] 2000-01."[6] Hip Hop's strong focus on knowledge and education in the late 80s and early 90s may deserve some of the credit for the rise of aspiring African American teachers during that time.

Hip Hop's Civil War

It is no wonder that a culture which was born in the streets where gang battles were once fought, has in its DNA the capacity to produce saber-toothed MCs and spark sibling rivalries like what happened between the East and West Coasts in the mid 90's. But unchecked sibling rivalry can culminate in civil war. This was the volatile state of Hip Hop in my first college semester as I played that nostalgic game of 'name that tune.'

As the East Coast, West Coast rift died down and the lead protagonist from each side, Biggie Smalls and Tupac Shakur "died down" with it, rappers from both coasts realized that the beef was counter-productive. There was money to be made on the other side of the country, and so, in the spirit of capitalism something like a truce was called. But the Northeast originators of Hip Hop learned that the culture could not be contained to one region. This was okay as long as New York was still recognized as home base, to be respectfully tagged in some way if a rapper was going to cover all the bases on his way back to the bullpen. This was done in the intro to the song *Nas Is Coming*, released just as the east-west beef began to thaw. In it, Dr. Dre appears, representing the best of the West Coast (music) and Nas represents the East Coast (known for rap skills). After acknowledging one another as untouchable, innovative leaders, the bottom line is drawn:

Nas : I'm tired of Niggaz stealin' beats, stealin' your whole technique

Dre : It's like this, Niggaz can't do it like I do it...just like Niggaz can't do what you do. You know all these Niggaz out here just talkin this East coast, West coast bull-s***, Niggaz need to kill that s*** and make some money....Let's get together and make some f***ing music...and get paid, and let's just let that be it.

Nas : Word...that's what I'm sayin

While Dre was tagging home base, Nas was giving up a base. This was a time in his career when Nas struggled to be consistent with his Conscious rap aspirations. He could have squashed the east-west beef in the name of unity, or peace, or to set an example for youth, or because TWO many lives had been lost. But, not knowing what was looming on Hip Hop's horizon, Nas squashed the beef in the name of capitalism. This would come back to haunt him and the entire East Coast.

While all of this was happening, evidence was beginning to bud that Hip Hop's seeds had not just been scattered across the country from east to west, but had also been blown toward the boarders at the bottom of the map. The South, Hip Hop's "Third Coast," began to make the kind of noise that would reverberate throughout the rest of the country and catch the ear of the mainstream. Artists such as OutKast, Goodie Mob and Master P were among the first to garner attention from the rest of the nation. Around the turn of the century one could feel the difference in the Hip Hop air.

After Biggie and Puffy had helped to break down the barrier of radio, the East Coast enjoyed a season of soaring on the airwaves. Artists such as DMX and Jay Z flew high with Swizz Beats as they beat their wings on these fair winds. But increasingly, the skies were becoming crowded with fly artists from the South and Midwest such as Birdman with the Cash Money Millionaires, and The St. Lunatics which gave us Nelly. Even southern rappers would look to tag the NY base with a nod of respect as one southern rapper put it, "I represent the [Atlanta] A's but still I spit it like a Yankee."

Northerners braced for the culturally cold winter as Hip Hop spread its wings to fly south. Many voiced their displeasure with the new direction of the culture but some eventually gave in to the new season. In 2006, after migrating to Atlanta, New York rapper Fat Joe teased, "Why is everybody so mad at the South for? He challenged rappers to changer styles and "switch to southpaw." This regional shift was different than the schism that surrounded the deaths of Biggie and Tupac.

Instead of recording artists, the frowns and fights were coming from consumers and Hip Hop enthusiasts. Northerners complained of a sickening sense in the gut, like parents feel when watching their child take an unsupervised journey to an unfamiliar part of town. What was Hip Hop doing going way down south and would it know how to make its way back home? However, the South, expressed a certain exuberance, like the surprising joy of gaining or winning something extremely valuable or unexpected; like your team winning the Super Bowl on Christmas!

The South began to experience what the North had known for years – homegrown Hip Hop that everyone else had to respect (or at least accept). Remember our earlier point of caution about one generation not finding beauty in what another might? Well, here was a case in which one region, the North, was struggling to appreciate the artistic beauty of another region, Hip Hop's South, with its infatuation with infectious hi-hats and gaudy, gold teeth.

But this was simply a role reversal; for years, those in the South and Mid-west struggled to identify with what was coming out of the Northeast in the name of urban culture. Christian rapper, Flame, of St. Louis once admitted, "We used to watch videos and see dudes from New York with big coats and Timberland boots standing on the corner and we just couldn't relate." In a tribute to The Cross Movement, the Philly/Jersey based rap group of which I was a part for 14 years, Flame spells out one of the major differences between his region and mine. He rapped, "We liked our beats fast, they liked their beats slow/ they rep'd Christ over beats that was East Coast."

The new music from the "Dirty South" and Midwest had one advantage over East Coast rap; something that, in its origin, Hip Hop was fueled by – dancibility. This was music that made you move! And this gave southern Hip Hop another advantage – clubability - entrance onto the club scene, not just for a guest appearance at the top of the hour, but as V.I.P. And if something is a hit in the club, and a hit on the radio, then it is also a hit at the checkout counter. Sales charts increasingly told the story of southern rappers winning the hearts and wallets of the younger generation.

"Younger" was also another factor in the widening gap between North and South. A new generation was on the rise. Hip Hop generation 2 was busy being born in the mid 80s and early 90s, and was therefore unconscious during the height of the Conscious rap stage. When they came of age in the new millennium, even New York's youth enrolled in the "new school" of southern Hip Hop. No more soulful samples reflecting the struggle of African Americans; the younger could not relate to this. Instead, this new music was triumphant; symbolizing that the struggle was over.

The new millennial battle was just as much North vs. South as it was Old vs. New. This is why some first generation Hip Hoppers had a hard time expressing their issues. The concern was mainly that the next generation was seemingly being pioneered and perhaps, pirated by rappers who did not feel the need to "edutain" their listeners, and in some cases, did not appear capable of doing so even if the need was felt. Some were shocked to learn that leading southern rapper Lil Wayne had been a straight "A" student and yet his smarts rarely made it to his art. This was troubling to northeastern Hip Hoppers for several reasons which we must now discuss.

Hip Hop's Empty House

Though Hip Hop has had many stages besides Edutainment, somehow, even the "thug" in the North came across as an educator. The Notorious B.I.G. was received like a misguided Moses when he released his *10 Crack Commandments* which carried like utterances from a street-pharmaceutical prophet or lectures from a "legally blind" professor. Red Man's *How to Roll a Blunt* was an illicit infomercial that sounded like The Learning Channel had gotten into a big batch of "special brownies." In the North, there was a subconscious craving for consciousness and leadership. This can be seen by listening in on conversations in the North about the 'top 5 rappers of all time' (a common debate). The categories that northerners typically judge for are: writer/wordsmith; lyricist/communicator; charisma/personality; performer/public image; imagery/ story teller; changed the game/took us in a new direction; produced classics /gave us memorable, historic moments – all qualities that mark a leader. Biggie and Tupac were not just great artists; their artistry told us they were potential leaders. Their deaths were analogous to the death of King and Malcolm X for Hip Hop generation 1.

Whether he knew it or not, the rapper is a leader, essential for accomplishing one of two tasks: helping people get by and helping people get over. For blacks in the inner-city, race was once an anchor, keeping them from overcoming life's hurdles. The Civil Rights Movement fought to lower or eliminate hurdles that were unfairly propped up against blacks. But Hip Hop as a movement did not spend much time lowering the actual hurdles; instead, over time the culture developed two distinct "hops" in order to get over.

The North had primarily come to pride itself in what Nas called "Street-hop" where rappers get "props" for having their heads on straight, even if their morals are not quite as linear. What the South began to promote, (and not just the south but those from Hip Hop's second generation) could be termed "Strip-hop," where music is made exclusively for those on the drug-strip or in the strip-club without the slightest hint of justification. And as we have said, it was the, albeit juvenile, attempts to justify his actions that made the "thug" a little easier to bear than the raw "gangsta rapper." Nonetheless, it was the North's justification of the thug that paved the way for the wayward direction of Hip Hop as it traveled across the map.

It was rappers and respondents from the north who first

had a chance to pick up the mic/baton and get back on the mission of running/winning the race. Hip Hop was a marvelous gift, given to the inner-city just at a time when their voice could not be heard. But when the opportunity for personal success became clear, the idea of collective advancement was shelved in hopes of collecting an advance from the mint. The message and the people now have to wait until after enough rappers have used the culture to become rich.

It is like the father who works non-stop at the expense of his family and says to his secretary and colleagues, "I won't always work so hard, I just have to make enough money to retire, and then I will be with my family." Eventually he has an affair with his secretary but says, "this affair is just a fling. I won't always cheat on my wife, I just have to get this out of my system, besides, working so late every night for my family, I deserve a little reward, don't I?" Late one night he comes home to find his house empty, not of furniture, but of the family he claimed to be working so hard for. A note left on the coffee table informs him that his wife is divorcing him and has gone to be with another man who enjoys spending time with her and the children. She'll be sending for the furniture, soon the house will be empty of that too.

In the same way, when Hip Hop moved to the South, one could almost read the words of the "Dear John" letter on the coffee table at cafés, college coffee shops and open mic spots all across the country:

Dear (Sean) John*,

We've had some good times, I'll always remember them. But you know when I first met you I had dreams of uplifting a people. I don't think that's what you want anymore. Sometimes you still

---

* Sean John is the clothing and fragrance company of Hip Hop mogul Sean "Diddy" Combs *talk that conscious stuff, but mostly all you talk about is money. So, if that's what it's about, I'm headed south. If Booker T. Washington was right, I might be able to get more money down there anyway. But I don't know how long I'll stay; after all, I still do wanna uplift a people. If it doesn't work out, maybe I'll go back to where I was before we met, you always said I was a gift from God.*

One Love,

Hip Hop

P.S. I'll be sending for the children

I must admit, sometimes being a Hip Hop head from the Northeast feels like coming home to an empty house. Where is the next generation? Did we really waste precious time advancing ourselves instead of the people, all while telling ourselves that we were doing it "for the people?" In his single *H to the Izzo*, Jay Z claimed he was overcharging the music industry to make up for what was done to the Cold Crush Brothers early on in Hip Hop's history. But is this supposed to help the people or just Hip Hop? Is there a difference between the two? Is helping one the same as helping the other? It seems there two schools of thought on how to most accurately judge the health of Hip Hop. One view takes the pulse of Hip Hop, the culture. The other counts the sale of Hip Hop – the commodity. As we look down the other end of history's corridor, we see that these two views are not new at all.

Aurora Borealis – The Northern Lights

The first approach to measuring the health of Hip Hop is the "conscious rapper's" approach, which by way of extension, represents the traditional position of the North. This view is best stated by artist/actor Mos Def in his *Black on Both Sides* album intro, *Fear Not Man*:

People be asking me all the time, "Yo Mos, what's getting ready to happen with Hip Hop?" You know what's going to happen with Hip Hop? Whatever's happening with us....People talk about Hip Hop like it's some giant living in the hill-side coming down to visit the townspeople. We *are* Hip Hop, me, you...everybody. So, Hip Hop is going where we're going. So next time you ask yourself where Hip Hop is going, ask yourself, 'where am I going, how am I doing,' then you'll get a clear idea. So, if Hip Hop is about the people, and Hip Hop won't get better until the people get better, then how do people get better? Well, in my understanding people get better when they start to understand that they are valuable, and they're not valuable because they got a whole lot of money or because somebody thinks they're sexy but they're valuable because they've been created by God.

According to this view, the thermometer for taking Hip Hop's temperature is the holistic life of its people. Monetary success is downplayed while social and intellectual wellbeing and spiritual awareness is promoted. Like Du Bois, this is a "top down" approach to Maslow's hierarchy.

Some may argue that it is unfair or inaccurate to credit the entire northern region with holding to 'consciousness' as a means for measuring the health of Hip Hop and that this credit should go squarely to the "Conscious rap" branch. But there are two reasons why I believe we are correct in labeling it as the northern position. First, on his *Black Album*, Jay-Z had a *Moment of Clarity* in which he looked back over his career. Paying homage to the road he wishes he could have traveled he admits that if money was not so important to him, he would have rapped more like conscious rappers Talib Kweli and Common Sense, known for their skills and conscious content. He then humorously adds that after selling five million albums, it's clear that he has chosen another path.

Second, in 2006, Nas, who awkwardly walked the line

between the Conscious rap road and the sidewalk of "Street-hop," released an album lamenting that *Hip Hop is Dead.* When asked to explain this bold claim, Nas responded, "When I say 'Hip Hop is dead,' basically America is dead. There is no political voice. Music is dead...Our way of thinking is dead, our commerce is dead...." Nas continually turned the bright light of his interrogation against the younger generation as the murderers of Hip Hop for not knowing and honoring Hip Hop's conscious roots.

"Hip Hop is Dead." Was this pronouncement made prophetically or posthumously? That has been much debated. But no matter what the fact remains; Jay Z and Nas, the two icons who represent the face of Northeast Hip Hop, each in his own way put in a plug (or pulled the plug) in an attempt to elevate a more conscious version of the culture. The traditional northern stance is a firm, b-boy stance on the conscious concrete of Edutainment.

Aurora Australis – The Southern Lights

Coming out of the South, the other method for judging the success of Hip Hop can be summed up by the trendy T-shirt slogan seen on the swollen chests of southerners in response to Nas' "*Hip Hop is Dead*" claim. The shirts rhetorically read, 'If Hip Hop is Dead... why we still makin' bread?' These southerners repudiated Nas' claim and took it as a personal attack against their right to advance by the same means that northern rappers had employed for years. They felt that northerners were only complaining because rap's energy and earning potential was now catering to a foreign cadence. Hip Hop had not died, it simply moved south where historically the best machine for measuring the morality or heartbeat of anything concerning African Americans is the cash register.

It was now time for the South to shine as the new

messengers. But what would their *message* be? I would say, "Time will tell" but time has been telling for over a decade now. And Hip Hop's dream of uplifting a people seems further away than ever, especially as those who promise to "change the game" do nothing but continue to call the same old plays. Consider the following excerpts from an interview with Huston, Texas' TMI Boys:

> We're bringing back the struggle. Everything is the same story [just a] different day. Ninety-eight percent of the niggaz rapping come from the projects or some kind of hood. It's the same f***ed up story, ain't nothing new under the sun, so we're bringing back character.... There are too many rappers that ain't really saying too much... They're so redundant, trying to be too hard. I think the subject matters are dead, but as far as Hip Hop being dead you can't blame that on the South.... First of all, if Hip Hop is dead, then why are we making bread!? Everybody done had it, the East Coast has always had it, and then it went to the West Coast, the Midwest had for a minute... but they going to feel us and they gonna hear us.

And if you were to hear them, what would you hear? The "return of character?" The struggle of the people? Lamentably, their lyrics are too flagrantly foul to flash here: Women are objectified; self-worth is worn externally around the neck while internally neglected; the "hood" is hallowed as the unholy hangout of choice. Isn't this the same old **mess**age? It should be noted though that in this same interview, The TMI Boys confessed:

> Now I won't sit up here and say that I'm staying true to myself all the way through the record because this is the first record. The whole objective was [to] get in and make that music because we have the right people behind us, then we can turn around and... start talking about the Virginia massacre, Condeleeza Rice, and Bush.

Is this a promise of soon coming consciousness or merely for future civil complaints? We'll have to wait and see. Meanwhile, the culture continues to get colder and darker from the lack of the bright light of leadership. Jesus once told his followers, "You are the light of the world, so if the light that is in you is dark...how great will that darkness be?"* In other words, if the ones propped up and positioned to bring light, only bring more darkness, that would be a devastating darkness. Imagine coming home to a dark house and hearing a strange, frightening sound about five feet in front of you. Nervously, you inch your way over to the light switch and the moment you flick it on, the room instantly gets ten times darker. Emanating from the light bulb is a cold, murky blackness which spreads across the room as quickly as you hoped the light would. How perplexing? This happens whenever rappers promise light but then do not deliver, only to deliver more darkness instead.

Unclear Battle Lines

Sometimes having a conscience feels more like a burden than a blessing, and too often we ignore that inner voice of reason. Since many in the North had already been guilty of turning a deaf ear to conscious rappers, northerners reshaped their complaints against the South saying that the real problem was not just with the lack of consciousness, but with how the new generation only gave light to one stage of the culture. Other forms of the culture were needed for holistic wellbeing. Hip Hop generation 1 knew that you could not survive on a steady diet of the thug, the gangsta, Street-hop or Strip-hop without frequent medicinal measures of consciousness to breathe life back into the culture. Conscious rappers served as the inner-city's CPR as we walked the thin line between using the culture to make a killing and killing it softly. This understanding (or lack of it) clouded the atmosphere during an on-air debate between

---

* The Bible, Matthew 5:14; 6: 22, 23

legendary female MC /radio host Monie Love and new southern rap star (self proclaimed Trap-star = street hustler/ dealer) Young Jeezy during the Hip Hop is Dead debates:

Young Jeezy: I don't think Hip Hop is dead at all, it's just a new day and time, it's a new story...a new movement...you can't say that. This is the new millennium...

Monie Love: Honestly, I *can* say that. I can say that

Young Jeezy: This is for kids.

Monie Love: Honestly, I can say that the concept of Hip Hop is dead

Young Jeezy: I cannot say that. I can't say that or respect it.

Monie Love: Let me explain to you why I say that. I respect you enough to explain to you why I made my comment.

Young Jeezy: Ok, let's go

Monie Love: The reason why I say Hip Hop is dead, and nothing more than that, is because the original concept of Hip Hop is all different forms. You understand what I'm saying?

Young Jeezy: Ok

Monie Love: It's not just talking about one area of Hip Hop in as far as struggles, street hustlin' and coming up – which is a respected factor.

Young Jeezy: But Hip Hop is a way of Life.

Monie Love: Absolutely and I've been living it for 36 years Brotha, trust me I know!

Young Jeezy: So what I do is not Hip Hop?

Monie Love: That's not what I said Brotha.

Young Jeezy: So, it ain't dead then...

Monie Love: Yes it is!...Let me finish explaining to you...If there was more than one area of Hip Hop being given light, getting light, shining and all the rest of it, then Hip Hop would not be dead. Hip Hop is not just one concept; you know what I'm saying?

Young Jeezy: But who said it was? You got Nas, coming back saying Hip Hop is dead, who is he to say Hip Hop is dead?

Monie Love: Someone who's been here for a very long time.

Young Jeezy: What does that mean?[7]

In typical youth fashion, Jeezy could not accept the insight being offered by his elder. She especially lost him when, in an attempt to validate Nas, Monie Love appealed to Nas' longevity. This is the last thing that wins an argument with someone who's been around for a very short time and has somehow managed to be esteemed as a veteran in the game. As she laid out her case for what it would mean for Hip Hop to be "alive," Jeezy responded in a very American way, "You look at them first week numbers and we'll talk about it." First week numbers refers to first week album sales. Jeezy was saying in effect, "I'll show you Hip Hop is still alive; just watch my album sales." The T-shirt slogan strikes again. At that point, all of the on-air personalities erupted, "See, that's what's killing it, right there!"

But to Jeezy, his comment made perfect sense – all of the people who purchase his album will prove that there is a viable market called Hip Hop that is still alive. However, for Monie Love the case was just as clear. The market may be made up of people, but the market's health and the people's health are two separate things just like the tobacco industry which has raked in billions of dollars over the years. The health of the cigarette market in no way reflects the health of the people who consume that product. In fact the high success of the market was the direct cause of the poor health of the people. The sad truth may be that the high success of Hip Hop as a product may be directly linked to the unhealthy state of Hip Hop as a people.

In 2010, one of the freshest breaths to blow in Hip Hop in quite a while, Jay Electronica, rose as a potential cultural iconoclast. He hails from the South, but while homeless in New York, was enlightened by Five-percenters who were astonished by his northern approach to Hip Hop. In *Exhibit C*, he records their surprise: "It's quite amazing that you rhyme how you do and how you shine like you grew up in shrine in Peru." Jay had been a student of world religions and philosophy and was open to receiving the Five-percent Nation teachings as well.

Five-percent doctrine holds that eighty-five percent of the world is blind, ten percent is corrupt and the remaining five percent are the poor righteous teachers. His goal became to "civilize the eighty-fivers" and after learning the Five-percent lessons he announced, "I'm bringing ancient mathematics back to modern man." But Five-percenters will learn, like north-eastern colleges found in the 1800's, that studying ancient material for mental discipline instead of moral direction cannot reform. It is moral reformation, not formal information that we need. The "five-percent" concept, which originatcd in Harlem, NY in the 1960's, is likely a spin on Du Bois' talented tenth concept. Their concept of becoming "one" with the "Essence" through "knowledge" is also a spin-off of the Greek, Neoplatonic philosophical concept of "The One" being ultimate reality.

In stark contrast, in 2010, southern rapper T-Pain released a cartoon series about a house-party that was somehow turned into a ghost, named Freaknik. The ghost's mission was to liberate black youth, imparting a spirit of positivity and fun, minus morality. Freaknik's arch enemy in the cartoon is a group of northern, "elitist," talented blacks including Bill Cosby and Oprah Winfrey, following the views of W.E.B. Du Bois. The name of the group, the Boule, is fitting. Boule means "council of noble men" and was used to refer to members of Sigma Pi Phi, the nation's first African-American Greek lettered organization for educated professionals, founded in Philadelphia in 1904 when blacks were excluded from joining other professional associations.

Connecting the Dots

The North and South struggle continues: education vs. economics; consciousness vs. capitalism; a people to be inspired vs. a product to be invested in. As African Americans continue to live out these two approaches toward advancement, the 'powers that be' continue to put more money and muscle behind ideas that might make a profit but mostly maim and muzzle the people. The culture has been in trouble ever since *The Message* became marketable. At that point, for many, Hip Hop changed from an adjective to a noun. Before anything else Hip Hop was culture – a shared *way* of life. Culture is the "how" that describes a "what." Two different cultures may accomplish the same "what" through different "hows;" e.g. how we eat, develop clothing, esteem art and heroes, etc. But culture is not just about how we prepare food or parade fashion; it is about how we preserve family and perpetuate our future. Culture gives us the tools to accomplish these important tasks.

"Hip Hop is a *way* of life," goes the old saying. Life was the thing, Hip Hop was the way. But the culture has lost its sense of "what" and is now left with only the "how," and thus has become hollow. We have gone from young men standing around in ciphers in order to pass on our story and sharpen our oratory leadership skills to now having young men standing around in ciphers, on corners accomplishing much of nothing. Instead of our clothes distinguishing us as a unique culture and people, now they just distinguish us. And so, wearing the "wrong" colors or turning your hat to the "wrong" side in the "wrong" neighborhood can lead to death. The "how" has become the nonsensical "what." The tool has become the job; the way has become the thing; the adjective, a noun; the culture, a commodity; no people, just a product. Take your pick, Street-hop or Strip-hop. But we must now ask, with all of this hopping, who's really getting over, and who is getting over on whom?

Getting the Big Picture

1. Did northern Hip Hoppers ever have a legitimate reason to question the validity of southern Hip Hop? Why or why not?

2. Do rappers have any responsibility at all to use their lyrics and musical careers to lead a culture of people? Why or why not?

3. Do you see Hip Hop primarily as a good product or a people group?

4. In the "connecting the dots" section of this chapter, we talked about Hip Hop as simply *a way* to do things and not an actual thing to be done. What positive tasks could Hip Hop as a culture help us accomplish?

5 The Pyramid Scheme

P = People

$\mathcal{H}$ip Hop has certainly been presented as a means for urban youth to get over, but instead of getting over something, often the goal is to get over on someone. No one likes being scammed and everyone likes to think they would realize it if a scam was being pulled on them. But history is filled with stories of large numbers of people being conned as one man's pursuit of the American dream ends up creating another man's nightmare. Maybe we are all having the same American dream, only we are playing different roles in it. Some, not enjoying the dream, are hoping to wake up before things worsen while others snuggle comfortably, ignoring the alarm, hoping to experience a little more of the dream world their scams have created. But the alarm is getting louder and harder to ignore.

Scam #1

In 2008, when the U.S. economy collapsed, we saw America's ugly side. We felt firsthand the extent of Wall Street's extreme greed through companies like AIG and Bear Stearns' practice of "credit default swaps" which crippled the country. As the nation's financial foundation froze and then fractured, all types of scams and schemes were exposed; like the one pulled by Annette Yeomans. In March of 2009, 51 year old Annette surrendered at the Vista jail and was "booked" for investigation of grand theft and embezzlement to the tune of $9.9 million. She spent at least $240,000 on 400 pairs of shoes; $300,000 on designer clothing; 160 purses valued at $2,000 each. She also remodeled a bedroom in her home into a closet with a chandelier and a 32-inch TV. On a weekly basis, Yeomans would spend $25,000 on her personal credit card and then pay off the balance the following Monday with company funds. Meanwhile, the company was forced to lay off numerous workers due to lack of funds. One woman's dream became another man's nightmare.

Scam #2

How about Bernie Madoff? Late in 2008 the phrase "ponzimonium" was coined. This referred to the array of Ponzi schemes uncovered as the financial recession roared down the road that leads to Wall Street. A Ponzi scheme is when a broker of stocks or securities takes money from investors and claims to be investing it, but instead, he pockets the money. He only pays out as little or as much as is necessary to keep the scheme going. Of the many Ponzi schemes that were revealed in this period, Madoff's was the most infuriating. In fact, his may be the biggest Ponzi scheme in U.S. history. Bernie Madoff 'made off' with $65 billion in a scam that spanned over two decades. As long as there was a steady stream of new investors, and very few people requesting the money earned from their investment at the same time, the scheme continued undetected. It just so happens that the financial meltdown of 2008 destroyed both of those necessary conditions.

In December of that year, Madoff confessed his crime. He was arrested and in March of 2009, pled guilty to all eleven counts against him, including perjury, fraud and money laundering. He was sentenced to 150 years in prison. He and his wife's real estate and property were to be sold in order to return $171 billion dollars to share holders. His wife would be left with roughly $2.5 million and even that was attacked by angry investors.

Scam #3 – Closer to home

Ponzi schemes leave us feeling helpless because they are hard to detect until it is almost too late, making the money hard to recover. There is however, another type of scheme that is much easier to spot, which makes it all the more embarrassing when someone is caught in its clasps. This scheme hits closer to home for those of us who are not on Wall Street and perhaps, not even on Main Street. It is the classic, classless Pyramid scheme.

This works where one person at the top of the pyramid, often called the "pharaoh," gets a bunch of people underneath

him or her to buy into a product *or* an idea; for instance, a water filter or a license to sell water filters. The water filter is cheap. He will have to sell a lot of them in order to make money. However, the license to sell the water filters costs more because it comes with an added benefit. Anyone who buys the license now gets to sell licenses to new recruits. Each time a license is sold, a portion of the money goes to those who sit higher in the pyramid. The more people beneath you selling licenses, the more money you make and the higher you are in the pyramid.

Everyone cannot make it to the top. The masses are needed at the bottom to support the rise of others. Most pyramid schemes are equipped with fake testimonials and referrals to entice new bottom recruits. Can we compare elements of Hip Hop to this concept of a pyramid scheme? Let's see.

The Product

First, in a pyramid scheme, you need a product to sell. When it comes to Hip Hop, the product can be clothing, CDs, songs, or tickets to movies and shows of our favorite artists. In the age of file sharing and digital downloads, record labels and those at the top of the industry are watching sales of the product decline. Since so many artists have built their careers on glorifying criminal activity, they have no room to rebuke their fans for getting their music illegally.

This fear of hypocrisy was lost on Wu Tang Clan's Ghost Face Killah who, in 2008, was rudely awakened to the digital age. He rants, "I'm just saying [I have] 115,000 friends on the MySpace and I get like 30,000 [sales] or something like that in the first week, that's not good man, 'cause I know a lot of y'all got my [music], but y'all just downloaded it man. I'm asking y'all to go to the store and buy that."[1] The sale of Hip Hop as a product is waning, but what is still selling is the idea.

Form of Payment for the Idea

What is the big idea or the license behind Hip Hop and how does one buy into it? The idea seems to change depending on which version of Hip Hop we are talking about – the people or the product. But after observing the different stages of rap, it seems we are being sold competing ideas about the same seven questions; what is "Cool," "Manhood," "Womanhood," "Success," "Culture," "Family" and "who is qualified to define these things?" Buying into someone's idea gives you the right to represent those ideas to others. But unlike the product, you do not buy into the idea with money.

You buy in when you give the street level approval; the nodding of the head, the taking up of the trend, the tuning in to the frequency, the turning up of the volume; the cosigning of the concept. This benefits the scheme much more than buying a CD. A CD is like the water filter, someone has to sell a whole lot of them to make a profit. But if someone can get people nodding to, talking about, approving of and sharing their big idea, those people have just advertised and helped to sell something more important - the artist as an official distributor or licenser of ideas about 'cool, manhood, womanhood, success, culture and family.' The artist is selling himself as a baton – a leader.

Testimonials

Pyramid schemes are well equipped with fake testimonials and referrals. We see this in Hip Hop. We know that much of the glitz, glam, glow and girls in the videos are rented in order to entice us to buy into the product or idea. We have all heard of the rapper who intentionally gets sent to jail in order to have more street credibility; or rumors of rappers receiving flesh wounds from faithful friends in order to boast about being bulletproof. Maybe you've heard the common catchphrase from rappers like Cassidy, "Ask about me." And why should you ask about the artist? In order to be convinced that the product or the idea they are selling is "real." Some have even been caught in boldfaced lies trying to create the kind of referrals and testimonials that will help sell their scheme. One such case is that of Hip Hop crooner Akon, whose career is built on the idea that he sings with so much soul thanks to all the time he spent locked up in prison. On-line resource The Smoking Gun reported that his:

> Claims about his criminal career and resulting prison time have been, to an overwhelming extent, exaggerated, embellished, or wholly fabricated. Police, court, and corrections records reveal that the entertainer has created a fictionalized back-story that serves as the

narrative anchor for his recorded tales of isolation, violence, woe, and regret. Akon has overdubbed his biography with the kind of grit and menace that he apparently believes music consumers desire from their Hip Hop stars. Akon's invented tales appear to be part of a cynical marketing plan, but one that has met with remarkable success.[2]

Their words, "cynical marketing plan" amount to what we would call a perilous pyramid scheme. But, they admit Akon's plan has resulted in "remarkable success." They go on to list the fruits of his fabrication: "His Atlanta-area real estate portfolio alone is worth about $5 million. In January [2008], he paid $1.65 million for an 8697-square-foot McMansion... In February 2007, Akon and "Devyne" Stephens paid $2.65 million for a 13.29 acre Fulton County Estate."

If the ends justify the means, Akon's success may get him off the hook for lying. After all, it worked, didn't it? It may have put Akon higher up in the pyramid but what about the countless young people who fell for the scheme and bought into the idea that having a darker past is necessary for a brighter future?

How many CDs Do You Own?

Before the days of Ipods, you could easily tell what kind of music listener someone was by looking at their CD collection. But some people were not the type to buy CDs. Still, they were buying into artists ideas in other ways. They knew all the words and found ways to hear the music they wanted. They owned the music, maybe not the actual CD, but in their hearts and minds they had stored up all of their favorite songs. They were human Ipods, each with their own inner personal playlist. They thought they got away without paying for the music, but they still contributed greatly to the artist's success by paying compliments (oooh that's my song); paying attention (OMG is that So&So?); and paying homage (I love her; I can't wait to see her live in concert). It makes a tremendous difference when the right people buy-in in this way. But just who are the "right people?" The TMI Boys answer this in the same interview referenced above in chapter 4, saying:

> It does take a lot of money and power to get in this industry, if you don't have the streets, if you don't have no financial backing, if you don't have a hit song you ain't got s***. If you ain't got the streets [behind you], ain't any record labels checking for you. You're wasting your time. Even if the streets are behind you, but remember the streets do not buy records. So, you get the streets behind you and create that buzz for you and place you on the pedestal, but the objective is way bigger than that. You just use the streets for promotion and get the *other* people behind you; you get in and then you start selling to you know who and you know why.

Three things stand out from this interview. First, is the acknowledgement that the streets, meaning inner city youth and young adults, do not buy records as much as do people in other demographics. This leads to the second point, that even though "the streets" do not buy records, they are still a necessary part of the equation for success because they help to create a "buzz" and place artists on a "pedestal." In other words, it is when people in the streets, who don't even buy the product, go on to buy into the idea of a particular artist that other people are motivated to spend money and move the artist up higher in the pyramid.

This means that the artist with the new violent, vulgar hit song is not looking to get money from inner-city youth; he needs something much more valuable from them – their approval. Like the gladiator in the ancient Roman coliseum looks to the emperor to know whether or not he should give the deathblow to finish off his opponent; in the same way, inside industry execs and outside onlookers are looking to those in the streets to see whether a certain artist's idea (the latest version of Cool, Manhood, Womanhood, etc) should live or die. All this power lies in the hands of inner city youth. And sadly, the streets consistently give the thumbs up, granting life, to the things which injure and harm us, and thumbs down to that which could inject hope.

The third point that stands out is the "other people" the TMI Boys referred to in their interview. This was an allusion to a well known fact concerning who is really buying rap music. Once you "get in" with the streets, they said, you can "start selling to you know *who* and you know *why*." Who is the "who?" "The industry numbers are undeniable. A Sound Scan study once reported that 71 percent of rap music is purchased by white consumers."[3] But what may not be as safe to assume as some do is the "why."

Many authors and cultural critics look at the fascination of white youth with certain kinds of rap music and see a compulsory "consumption of black death." They say it has become culturally acceptable (and even pleasurable) for whites to hear about violence being done to blacks and that there is a subconscious craving for the obliteration of brown skinned people. But if this was the case, then the most ardent supporters of Gangsta rap music should be hate groups such as the Ku Klux Klan. But this is not so. Though it has become a social norm to see blacks as expendable, this does not require an appetite for such destruction; rather it merely explains the acceptance of it.

I believe the TMI Boys come closer to helping us understand the fascination of whites with black culture. "You know who" doesn't initiate the process. In actuality, "you know who" doesn't get involved until they see the streets get behind an artist and put someone on a pedestal. The streets have become the authenticators and legitimizers of the concept of "cool." It seems elementary and almost anti-intellectual to suggest that what it all boils down to is social curiosity and pure peer pressure; the desire to be in the in-crowd where the action is. But history will show this to be the case.

In the next chapter we will see that this phenomenon goes back to the origins of Rock & Roll. But for now, consider that rather than having a morbid appetite for "black death," it is more likely that we have been witnessing a strong desire from white youth to participate in black life. And for our own selfish, confused reasons, the only life we are supporting and showing off for others to participate in happens to be, our own demise. I say this because even though 71% of Hip Hop music is purchased by whites, certainly over 71% of it is actually lived out by non-whites.

Life Deserves a Score

Gone are the days of being able to look at someone and simply assume that they listen to a certain type of music. In the age of the internet, music cannot be said to be specific to one "culture." However, it is interesting that there is hardly a culture in the world that does not have a form of music to colorfully express the life and matching emotions of its people. Music serves as a soundtrack to our lives. Introducing the 'musical accompaniment' category at the 2009 Oscar Awards, actor Hugh Jackman underscored the importance of a musical score when he was tele-prompted to say, "A movie without music is like a plane without fuel." Planes without fuel don't fly, they don't even take off. In the same way, the soul without a song struggles to soar. We make up music in our own heads if we have to because life, with all of its beauty, misery and complexity, deserves a score.

Music and movies were never really separate to begin with. The Greeks, from whom we get our modern form of theater, used to produce seasonal plays, tragedies and comedies in which the actors did not talk with their own voices. Instead, there was a chorus along the side of the stage that sung whatever needed to be said throughout the course of the play. These plays were designed to make the audience feel a great deal of complex emotions and then experience what they called 'catharsis.' This was a sort of emotional cleansing that came from watching actors on stage go through a series of stressful scenarios. After this, it was believed the audience could go on with their own real lives more logically for a time, since all of their emotions had been released through this cathartic experience.

For their own reasons, they believed that a life full of passionate, emotional outbursts was not good. They believed stern logic, not emotion, should rule in regular life. One wonders what effect those emotional plays would have had on the Greeks had they produced them more frequently, perhaps daily, around the clock, all year long. Would it be like our modern media driven world? Would all that emotion without logic be too much for them? Is it too much for us?

Though we have surpassed the Greeks in the technical aspects of the production, they may have had one thing over our silver-screen, sterling-sound version of the amphitheater. In their plays, the catharsis came as whole crowds watched the main character miss out on blessings that would have come from living by the good virtues (e.g. honesty, bravery, loyalty, humility) and experience the burdens that come from giving in to the evil vices (e.g. dishonesty, cowardice, envy, pride). They wrote tragedies and even comedies demonstrating the way *not to* live in order to keep people from ending up like the tragic main character.

We, on the other hand, watch our particular programs to find out *how to* live and often imitate the main characters in some way. But we are not better off for this. Often, our good guys are a little bad; our bad guys are a little good. We cheer for the criminals and hope they get away with the money, the murder, the heists; we want them to get the girl at the end. We want their cars, their clothes, their budget - their lives. But we don't just want it; we believe they are helping us; somehow their songs and shows are showing us how to get it. The media loves that we look to them for this sort of self-help, a storyboard, a soundtrack. They tell us:

> "Just keep looking to the media, and like the Greek plays, you won't have to say anything original for yourself. Let all of the words come from the singers and rappers at the side of the stage. Sing along (or just move your lips) and soon all will be right."

In our society, the choir at the side of the stage has taken center stage. But has this really given us the help we need? Are our communities getting better the more we live to these soundtracks? Are we getting over, or is someone getting over on us? If we must have them, we must choose better soundtracks for our lives.

Hip Hop & the SELF Help Movement

Youth need to be empowered to see that they control a great deal of what happens in the scheme of modern media. They don't know it but they use that power every time they call the radio station to request their favorite song. Every time they answer the questions, 'who is your favorite artist?' or 'what is your favorite T.V. show?' on social networking sites. These are just some of the ways that individuals at the top of the pyramid find out how well the scheme is working and who the streets are "feeling" right now. The artists that youth praise become more visible, more viable and more valuable and they move more vertical in the scheme.

Many youth will never speak out against it because they don't see it as a scheme but as a successful strategy. A strategy that needs new success stories every so often which causes youth to think, "If I just polish up my product, maybe someday, they'll pick me to be the next testimonial and then I will 'come up.'" Because of this, many high school students who buy into the scheme feel that they do not have to prepare for life academically. They have bought into the media's idea of success and how success is attained. Most whites may buy into Hip Hop as a product in order to capture coolness, but most blacks buy into Hip Hop as an idea because for them it is found in the most popular isle of the store for the narcissistic soul – Self-help.

Think of some popular self-help books or audio CDs. It could be *12 Steps to Wealth and Fame*; *10 Keys to Loving Yourself Thin*; *What's So Great About You!* Or *Your Best Life Now*. These books promise financial, emotional and even spiritual success. The key to these self-help efforts is to get you repeating certain ideas to yourself in order to change the way you think about... you. If you can think of your personality, position, potential, and possibilities differently, then that mental change will begin to change your feelings and behavior and ultimately your reality.

The audio CDs are the most fun to watch people try out. Many movies have given us a dose of comedy by portraying the nervous job applicant going for an interview with earphones in ear, repeating some affirmation after a voice coming from an Ipod, "You are smart, talented and people like you. You deserve this job." They repeat, "I am smart, talented and people like me. I deserve this job." Self-help books and CDs are not necessarily a waste of time. There are some that offer quite a bit more than pleasant affirmations. Some actually give action steps as to how one can address personality issues, cope with or change their position in life while maximizing potential and creating new possibilities. There are others, however, that promise progress and change but lack the precision to produce such a result. Meanwhile, the authors are raking in the dough.

How does Hip Hop compare to this? The next time you're walking or driving down a city block, look for the youngster walking along, with or without earphones in ear, rapping to him or herself the lyrics from a song that talks about success in some way, possibly in some illegal way. If you can, ask this individual, "Why are you singing those lyrics to yourself and what is it doing for you?" Hip Hop music has become a series of sonic self-help sessions where those who buy-in believe they are being helped to see their personality, position, potential and possibilities differently than when they awoke this morning.

If someone is not as tough as he thinks he should be, he can meditate on some Gangsta rap. If he needs help in dealing with the opposite sex, he has a playlist full of Strip-Hop. If he has not had a real man show him how to grow out of boyhood, he can copy the swagger of a popular artist. If a young lady has questions about the butterflies she gets in her stomach every time she sees a certain boy, don't worry, there is a new song from an R&B diva that will sing her a solution. And if that boy begins to cheat on her, the same artist has a tune for that as well. If someone begins to sense that there is some design to the world or that there is a systematic effort to negatively impact their community and they want to feel as if they are doing something about it, they can recite some Conscious rap lyrics. Meditating on and repeating these words, just might help us become all that we can be.

Remember, self actualization is the highest level of Maslow's hierarchy. The term "actualization movement" is also another name for the self-help movement. What is the connection between the self-help movement and Maslow's hierarchy which starts at the bottom and demands that we work our way up to actualization? Well, for starters, the self-help movement aims to assist people with reaching the top level of Maslow's order. But more interesting is the fact that, both the movement and the hierarchy result in only a few well-off people at the top, and a host of not-so-well off individuals at the bottom. Therefore, both fit nicely into the structure of a pyramid scheme. In his book *Sham: How the Self-help Movement Made America Helpless*, Steve Salerno introduces the acronym S.H.A.M. which he says stands for the Self Help and Actualization Movement. The highest level of Maslow's hierarchy is actually "Transcendence" which has to do with helping others to reach actualization. This level is often forgotten because working from the bottom up, so few people ever reach it.

Connecting the Dots

How could someone determine whether or not their particular brand of Hip Hop is a sham? One of the best ways would be to look at others around you who have bought into the product or idea of a particular artist and ask yourself, how is the listener really being helped? If you realize that the artist is getting more out of the deal than you are and you find that you are having the hardest time reproducing what the artist is advertising in your own life, it's very likely that you have bought into a pyramid scheme – self-help that will not help you. In chapters 10 and 14 we will discuss forms of Hip Hop where the success and lifestyle the artists promote is just as accessible to the listener as the performer.

Sadly most forms of Hip Hop qualify as a scam. The money travels up the chain," while those at the lower levels are left with fashion, dance moves, soundtracks, swagger, and memories, but no real results as the people tend to get worse helping the product get better.

Epilogue - You Call That a Baton?

Now the nasty nature of the scheme becomes visible. In the first chapter we discussed how the baton, which was meant to pass between the Civil Rights generation and those who followed, was disrupted by violence. Leadership was lost, left laying somewhere on the track and field of African American history. Since then, a new baton has been fashioned and handed to the next runner. But this new baton is the very thing that Du Bois would have fought and Washington would have forged in Tuskegee.

The baton is "self-help" with the goal of actualization that must start out at the bottom of Maslow's hierarchy. While capitalism is failing in America, economists are struggling to prove that it was not a sham all along. Meanwhile, the self-help pyramid scheme is destroying culture and eroding family. This scheme has always worked against the youngest among us and continues to stunt the growth of each generation that buys in to it. To see this, in the next section, we will examine the links between capitalism, the creation of the American teenager and the breakdown of the American family.

Getting the Big Picture

1. When Hip Hop becomes simply a product, what do the "people" actually get out of it?

2. Does the version of Hip Hop that you most often encounter qualify as a pyramid scheme? If so, how? If not, why?

3. If so, what part do you play in the scheme? Are you buying into the product, the idea, selling the product or selling the idea?

4. Have you ever tuned into Hip Hop for self-help?

5. If so, did it help you and how so?

Part Two

Between
Hippies & Hip Hop

6 Why Must I Be a Teenager?

*I*n the 1950's Dion and the Belmont's sang the popular tune, *Why Must I Be a Teenager In Love?* But we have a more interesting question to consider, 'why must I, or anybody, be a teenager in the first place?' It sounds like a trick question doesn't it? Anyone who is in their teenage years is obviously a teenager, right? Well that depends; not on the year of life a person is in, but on the year in which the question is being asked. The term "teen" or "teenage" was used as an adjective since 1921.[1] But the word "teenager" did not appear as a noun in our written language until 1941.[2] There is a world of difference between using a word to simply describe something and using that same descriptive word to fully define a thing.

In creative writing, we are taught that strong nouns should always replace weak adjectives. For instance, calling a chandelier very bright is weak; comparing it to the sun, is strong. Saying, "he drives that fireball" is stronger than saying, "he drives that strikingly red car." But we have done the exact opposite by turning the weak adjective "teenage" into an even weaker noun, "teenager." The noun is weak, but we will see that the people it refers to are certainly not.

Before the Teen Age

If the word "teenager" only began to define youth as recently as 1941, then what were youth known as before then and what led to this change? Author Milton Mertzer has an answer to the first question: *Cheap Raw Material*. Meaning, America's rich success with capitalism was not just built on the free labor of African slaves but on the cheap labor of white children. As far back as the 1700's, children worked in America, often for twelve to sixteen hours a day. White youth in England, were routinely nabbed against their will and shipped off to America to be sold as cheap young laborers. We get our term "kidnapped" from this part of history. We will see that capitalism, along with evolution's "survival of the fittest" dogma which fueled Maslow's bottom up hierarchy, has been pushing white youth and African Americans into the same boat long before Hip Hop.

Not every child worker was forced into service. In 1835 Harriet Hansen went to work full time in a spinning mill at the tender age of ten because she wanted to "earn money like the other little girls"[3] Many youth and some parents actually preferred children earning over learning. Eleven year old Lucy Larcom wanted to go to school but her $1 per week job could help the family more.[4] Children worked in fields, farms and factories for pennies per day. The working conditions and sometimes the work itself were hazardous to one's health. Picture eleven year old boys in cotton mills losing fingers to greedy machines; working in temperatures of up to 115 degrees Fahrenheit with the windows nailed shut to keep the proper moisture needed for the cotton. Mertzer gives two startling accounts of the conditions in which children worked; the first – children making bricks from clay:

> I went down to a brickfield and made a considerable inspection. I first saw, at a distance, what appeared like eight or ten pillars of clay.... I found to my astonishment that these pillars were human beings. They were so like the ground on which they stood, their features were so indistinguishable, their dress so soiled and covered with clay that, until I approached and saw them move, I believed them to be products of the earth....Moreover, the unhappy children were exposed to the most sudden transitions of heat and cold, for after carrying their burdens of wet clay, they had to endure the heat of the kiln, and to enter places where the heat was so intense that I was myself able to remain no more than two or three minutes.[5]

And the second – chimney sweeps:

> Forced screaming and sobbing up dark, narrow chimneys, their skin
> scorched and lacerated, their eyes and throats filled with soot, these
> small children...faced suffocation in the blackness of a chimney or
> perhaps a slow and painful death from cancer of the scrotum, the
> climbing-boys' occupational disease. Of all unhappy child-workers
> these were perhaps the most ill-used and forlorn.[6]

In the city, things were somewhat better, not just for
white youth, but black children as well. "The city offered so
much work that a kid could quit or get fired from one job and
find a new job within hours. African-American children, often
excluded from textile mills and factories, found work
opportunities in the city."[7] In the late 1800's and early 1900's,
children as young as seven were working on city streets as
newspaper boys and boot blacks. A 1920 U.S. census reported
that 20,513 newsboys between the ages of six and ten were
working on the streets and some as young as five.[8] When asked
why the children wanted to work, only twenty-eight percent
listed money as a factor. Most responded that there's nothing
else to do, it's fun to hustle and that it's no fun just playing
around.[9] Some parents even tried to bribe their youth with
money to go to school instead, but the children wanted to work
like their friends.

What changed? Many parents had been complaining for
years that by working children were not learning progressive
skills for steady employment.[10] But nothing changed. The
children themselves frequently organized strikes to demand
better working conditions. These youth were certainly not weak
nouns; they were not "teenagers." They wore the chains of
capitalism, sometimes physically as harsh as slavery, only
without the psychological torture attached. They fought and
conditions changed from horrible to bad, but overall not much
changed. In the early 1900's a group of political activists known

as the Progressives began to fight for labor laws that would move children out of harm's way. The Child Labor Act of 1916 made the state-to-state sale of products produced by children under certain ages illegal, crippling certain industries. For the first time the United States had decided to protect America's working children.

But this victory was short lived. After two years of employers complaining that the government had overstepped its lawful limits, the Supreme Court overturned the law. Other laws were passed as well in an effort to protect children in and from the workplace but were likewise overturned. Factory and mill owners claimed that the industries would go bankrupt if children didn't work. They also said that families and society would suffer from an increase in "crime, wickedness, and pauperism."[11] Although wrong in their treatment of children, they may have had a point.

In the 1930's, over 625,000 boys and girls ages ten to fifteen were working in the United States.[12] But this was the decade of the Great Depression. President Franklin D. Roosevelt had to find a way to address the nation's dying economy and countless unemployed adults. To do this, he struck a "New Deal" with the American people, part of which involved freeing up jobs for adults by limiting children's right to work. The conservative judges on the Supreme Court, known for caving in to businesses that thrived on of the cheap labor of children, may not have gone for such liberal laws; but in his second presidential term Roosevelt was able to appoint a few of his own justices to the Bench.

Together, they passed the Fair Labor Standards Act of 1938, which raised the age at which a child could work to sixteen in most cases; limited the types of jobs someone under the age of eighteen could work; and limited the hours a child could work so as to not interfere with school. It would be wonderful to say that America finally stood up and did the right thing, but we must remember that it was not just the ethical but the economical and political stress that made America change its laws. The ethical concerns had been ignored for several centuries in favor of capitalism. But now capitalism needed the jobs of the nation's youth. The strong yet powerless hurting children were only released because the more powerful, voting adults were now hurting.

Three years after this, these strong children officially became known by that very weak noun. "Teenager" is weak because it only tells us the age range of an individual, but nothing specific. It tells us what a person cannot do legally, but it does not tell us what a person can do. Before these laws passed, people in their teenage years could be distinguished by various interests and occupations. But afterwards, they could be lumped together with one common characteristic - idleness, no occupation. They were indistinguishable, invisible, silenced - "teenagers."

The Curse and the Blessing...and the Curse

Could losing the right to work really be considered a curse? Children could still go to school to keep occupied and keep their hands and minds busy. But there is an enormous difference between being occupied and having an occupation; between being kept busy and tending to one's own business. With work, there is an immediate benefit, a paycheck. With school, there is delayed gratification, where benefits and rewards are not just around the corner; they are around the corner, across the street, and up the block; further in the future than we can see at the moment. Many of the good things in life operate on this principle but it is hard enough for adults to grasp the idea of delayed gratification, let alone for youth. Granted, in the 1940s and 50s they did not have microwaves, cell phones and remote controlled everythings, so the concept of delayed gratification would not have been as foreign to them as it is to us. At any rate, this was a lesson the "teenager" was forced to learn. But how well would they learn it?

Growing up in the 1980s I had the pleasure of watching re-runs of two very old black-and-white TV shows about children. Back then I could not understand why these shows seemed to be extreme opposites of one another. Now it seems that this was just a case of Hollywood shuffle. The first show was produced before the Fair Labor Act of 1938. During the 1920s and 30s America was often entertained by the antics of *Our Gang* or *The Little Rascals* as they were later legally called. *The Little Rascals* is credited with being the first major Hollywood production to put white males, blacks and females all on an equal plane and for doing so at a time when both blacks and women were treated as second class citizens.

But the show did something else. Through a bit of reverse psychology, it helped America feel good about young working children. Instead of dealing with the reality that young people were slaving in grueling jobs, the show's children were shown spending their time in the streets, getting into minor neighborhood mischief. It was as if to say to parents, "What would you prefer: your small children to be productive by working or for them to be outside drifting and draining society like these little rascals?" Many of the forty-one child actors who played and replaced various roles throughout the life of the show stayed just as long as they looked young enough to fit with the show's theme. However, after around age twelve, they were no longer needed. No one needed to be convinced that teenaged people should be working since "by 1914, every state but one had a minimum working age of at least twelve."[13] A show about idle "teenagers" on the street would not have made much sense.

After the 1938 labor laws however, things got a lot more interesting for the non-working teenager. Hollywood once again shuffled out a show in order to help America accept what capitalism was doing to the nation and to youth. In the 1950s the first TV show that attempted to look at life from a teen's point of view, *Leave it to Beaver,* was produced. The show tried to answer the question, "If those little rascals are no longer cute lil' ragamuffins running the street, but are now in their teen-aged years and unable to work because of the new laws, then what are they doing with all their time and energy?" An honest answer to this question might have saved America from what was to come. But since the country was now prospering, and the backbone of a prosperous nation is believed to be the middle class, Hollywood zoomed the lens in on the middle class family with the creation of the Cleavers (Beaver's family).

The Cleavers were the ideal mid-20th century family, with Ward, the father, working and June, his wife, a stay at home mom. Beaver's older brother, Wally, was a respectable young man with middle class swagger, while Beaver was a charming little guy who had a knack for getting into minor league trouble due to his "teenager" curiosity and naiveté. This is the way America wanted to picture its idle youth; young and dumb, but also cute and content enough to go to school, come home, and wait for adulthood while leaving the gainful employment to the "grown-ups." But unfortunately, that was TV. In real, unscripted life, the only good this did was to help adults feel better about sentencing youth to 16 years of no labor in a prison called "teenager." Youth in other nations, and some proactive youth in America, get through the education process in much less time and become productive in society. They never get used to idleness as a way of life, the never become "teenagers."

The Blessing

"Idle hands are the devil's workshop," goes an old saying. But the idleness introduced to the youth of the 1940s and 50s was not entirely unproductive or unprofitable. In fact, it led to the creation of something that America has profited from ever since – youth culture. In the late 1940s, Jazz, Gospel and Blues music had been successfully combined into what began to be called 'Rock & Roll.' The music that laid the foundation for Rock & Roll was at first labeled 'race music' and was not played on white radio stations. This musical, racial separation was held until the mid 50s when the idleness of white youth produced the curiosity which led many to venture across the color line. This was dramatized by the stage and screen production *Hairspray*.

Some whites did not have to go as far as actually listening to black artists in order to hear and have black music. A number of white singers and bands coveted and covered black music, recording their own versions of the same songs, sometimes illegally. Eminem draws on this historical backdrop when he jokes about himself and Hip Hop on his 2002 single *Without Me*, calling himself, "the worst thing since Elvis Presley, to do black music so selfishly," using it to get himself "wealthy." The emerging youth culture of the 1950s began to drive a wedge between white parents and youth. Parents could not understand why their youth were listening to *that* music, and youth were beginning to suspect the values of their parents who they now saw as potentially being wrong on the race issue.

Many new lessons were being learned in the same semester of this real life social studies class. While all of this was happening with music, major changes were being made on the legislative level. In 1954, the landmark Supreme Court case of Brown v. The Board of Education, ruled that 'separate but equal' segregation laws, (in place since the Supreme Court case of Plessy v. Ferguson in 1896), were inherently unjust. As long as public facilities were separate for whites and blacks, they would almost certainly be unequal in quality. Schools were forced to desegregate.

White parents were outraged; black parents were

astonished; while black and white youth tried to remember the dance floor choreography as they would now have to learn to rock and roll together in real life. It would take something grittier than *Grease Lightning* to grease the wheels of this transition. Far from the Lilly-white lens of the *Leave it to Beaver* camera crews, America's youth culture was budding and bubbling with new ideals as idleness gave way to an iconic industry. Those who were around and aware witnessed the changing face of America from mature steel to the face of youthful zeal.

...And the Curse

The idleness of youth did not produce strictly favorable results. Unlike wholesome Wally and 'the Beave,' much of American art and film bears witness to the growing unrest of youth in the 50s and 60s. The popular Broadway musical *Westside Story*, Susan Eloise Hinton's *The Outsiders*, and movies like *Grease*, all depict the life of the "teenager" in the 50s and 60s as something with very dark and foreboding clouds; a middle-passage   between childhood and adulthood where it is understood, 'some may not make it.'

These artistic depictions show that many youth were beginning to question the traditional ideas handed down to them concerning things like race, and the importance of a person's economic or social status. Those things were deeply important to their parent's generation but youth were discovering that these were merely personal preferences and opinions, not absolute statements of fact that will always be true no matter what - we call these "absolutes." Teens began to wonder, "Have adults confused opinions with absolutes while we as 'teenagers' are able to tell the difference between the two?" This was a dangerously significant discovery because as things progressed, teens became increasingly suspect of the moral values of parents and politicians, and eventually began to distrust much of what they had learned from them. "What else," teens wondered, "have these adults passed off as an 'absolute truth' that really is nothing more than mom and dad's opinion?" This suspicion laid the groundwork for a new kind of thinking; a philosophy that has dominated and deconstructed much in American culture over the past 40 years.

Postmodernism and Absolutes

Postmodernism and relativism came into vogue in the 70s. It grew as a reaction to religious dogmatism and scientific empiricism, both of which claim to have a trustworthy approach to determining the "absolutes" in life – religion as it pertains to truth and science as it pertains to facts. Postmodernism rejects both of these and sets up each individual's own intuition as the only trustworthy guide to truth; not *absolute* truth, but *relative* truth for each person and them alone. In an attempt to get away from people's opinions which have been passed off as "truth," postmodernists deny any type of absolute statement and approach everything as "that's what you say," or "says who?"

Postmodernism has three possible opponents: first, because people are prone to mistake opinion for truth, postmodernism questions the person speaking – this is a challenge of *authority*. Next, postmodernism may have a problem with the truthfulness of a statement being made at any given time – this is a challenge of *actuality*. Lastly, instead of taking issue with the source of authority or a statement's actuality, postmodernism may challenge the *angle* something is being approached from; which sounds something like this:

"I understand what you're saying and maybe that's true for you, but you cannot say that what's true for you is true for everyone else. You can only speak personally from your own point of view. There is no one objective truth for us all; there is only subjective truth for each person."

If you've grown up in America anytime from the 1970s onward you've been influenced by postmodernism. If you've ever used the words, "What's true for you is true for you and what's true for me is true for me" or "there is no absolute truth." That's pretty much the postmodern motto word for word.

At first this seems like a very loving way to live and let live, but just think for a moment and this becomes quite questionable. For example, if you were to give me a $20 bill and ask for change, suppose "change" for a $20 to me is two $5s, but to you it is two $5s and a $10? Would you accept my two $5s if I were to tell you,

"Hey, don't try to put your 'absolute' ideas on me; there are no absolutes! To you, change for a $20 is one thing, but to me it is another. What's true for you is true for you and what's true for me is true for me."

That simply would not work. You would tell me that there is absolutely such a thing as change for a $20 (like two $5s and a $10) and there are other things that are absolutely not change for a $20 (like two $5s). Postmodern reasoning will not work in a case such as this.

As chaotic as this seems, we must remember where this way of thinking stems from. Postmodernism came on the scene at a time when young people did not feel they had the freedom to challenge their parent's views head-on. Instead, they chose the non-confrontational, passive aggressive approach of changing the language and landscape of "right" and "wrong." By allowing those words to have different meanings for different people, they could escape the burdensome task of having to prove parents wrong about such things as race or morality. Without absolute truth or meaning, parents and youth could be right at the same time even though they completely disagreed.

The good thing about this new way of thinking was that it created common ground between people who might never have agreed otherwise due to someone's narrow minded view. Take for example a prejudiced father in the 1970s who would not allow his daughter to date someone of another race. If that prejudiced father suddenly became a postmodern thinker, he would be forced to say to his daughter, "Hey, whatever is right for you is right for you." This would be good. However, there is a down side to it. Because postmodernists avoid almost all forms of 'absolute right' or 'absolute wrong' language, the prejudiced-turned-postmodern father could not object to anything at all, even if the daughter claimed to be in love with and engaged to the tree in the front yard. Dad must accept this because there is no absolutely right thing and no absolutely wrong thing. The postmodernist rejects everyone's position, but strangely, also has to accept everyone's position at the same time because "what's true for you is true for you and what's true for me is true for me."

To make matters worse, because there is no qualified reason for the postmodernist's acceptance of one thing or rejection of another, they end up belittling and demeaning every idea they happen to accept. For instance, if the white, prejudiced-turned-postmodern father now accepts his daughter's black boyfriend, but not because the boyfriend is a person made in God's image, but only because no one can say what is right or wrong for another person, then the father has not changed for the better, he has changed for the worse. He has not come to value the black boyfriend; instead he has leveled everything by raising the value of certain things and lowering the value of others so that no one thing is better than anything else. The black boyfriend, the tree out front, it's all the same. There is no longer any such thing to him as absolute truth, value, meaning, right or wrong.

Pseudo Psychology and Psychedelic Pharmaceuticals

You might be asking,

"Okay, maybe we think this way sometimes today, but what kind of mindset did people need to have in order to adopt this way of thinking at first? And how were people able to live with this bizarre world-view?"

We must keep in mind several things. First, postmodernism is not totally bad. It paved the way for pluralism, which guarantees the acceptance of many different viewpoints. But in those days, people had not yet learned the art of pluralism. The sad thing is that today, we have perhaps learned it too well. A proper pluralism says something like, "Maybe I don't believe you're right, but that doesn't mean that you don't have rights." This is what we call, "tolerance." But pluralism practiced under the rule of postmodernism says, "All of us are right; even though we all disagree." This is what we might call "nonsense." If we are all right, and we disagree, then we are also all wrong. This is why even today the disclaimers "like" and "or whatever" are an important part of youth speech. They don't know why but they are afraid to make definite statements about anything in life.

This new way of thinking was helped along by new shifts in the secular world. In the field of psychology, college students were being taught humanistic theories, like Carl Rogers' person-centered approach to psychotherapy which says that reality is less important than each individual's experience of it. Another key moment was the 1969 publishing of Thomas Harris' popular self-help book *I'm OK, You're Ok*, which fueled the idea that right and wrong is something that each person had the ability to determine for themselves form about ten months old.[14] Philosophers had long since been looking for a way to rid the human heart of ancient, religious models of morality and it just so happened that this idle and suspicious teenaged generation was the perfect guinea pig for the postmodern ethical experiment.

The American "teenager" was beginning to nurse on the nauseating nectar of anarchy. The full blown expression of personal freedom we see so much of today comes as a direct result of youth in the late 60s to mid-80s rebelling against the social order. The term 'rebel without a cause' came into vogue during that period because many young people were rebelling just to know that they could. Many of these same rebels often regretted their rebellion once they experienced the limited joy and unlimited chaos that came along with too much freedom.

The classic 1985 song *Everybody Wants to Rule the World* by Tears for Fears displays the bewildering effects of growing up in a "teenager's" world, bound by too much freedom. In it, they confessed that living by "my own design" leads to "my own remorse." They begged for help with deciding how to "make the most of freedom and of pleasure." But why did they need help? Because everyone deciding what was right in their own eyes had led to a "lack of vision;" and left them feeling like, "everybody wants to rule the world." Many sang the song, but missed the fact that these young adults in the 1980s were crying out to be delivered from the freedom and anarchy of the 60s.

There were two other factors that led to the adopting of the postmodern philosophy. As youth rejected their parent's values and morals, questioning their parent's faith was a natural outcome. Many opened their minds to embrace Eastern Mysticism, Hinduism and Buddhists beliefs. This newly found religious attitude from the East introduced the idea of many gods and pluralism into the American consciousness.

The second factor was the introduction of psychedelic drugs. Just like Hip Hop began with Cool Herc's mobile party machine in the mid 70s making its way around the neighborhoods of the Bronx, in the mid 60s there was a different type of mobile party machine making its way across American neighborhoods. This machine was a school bus named "Further," driven by Ken Kesey and the Merry Pranksters. In 1959 Kesey volunteered as a guinea pig for a CIA sponsored study on the effects of psychedelic drugs such as LSD (commonly called "acid") and cocaine. Several years later he teamed up for a cross country road trip with others who had taken to the lifestyle of the budding hippie culture. The hippie movement swelled amongst mainly white middle class youth who did not take the *Leave it to Beaver* approach to teenaged life. They rejected much of the commercial, materialistic outlook on life which they saw in their parents' generation.

At festivals around the country, rock music, which progressed from Rock & Roll, was becoming synonymous with the growing hippie crowd, along Ken Kesey's contribution. As he traveled the country on that now famous road trip he spread the psychedelic drug aspect of the hippie movement, conducting "acid tests" which "turned on" curious bystanders to the altered or "higher" consciousness that came from LSD through what they called "acid trips." Timothy Leary, a Harvard professor at the time, did the same in numerous research studies conducted under his care at the university. LSD had not yet been declared a controlled substance; therefore this "experimentation" was legal. In July of 1967, *Time* magazine featured a story describing the hippie code, "Do your own thing, wherever you have to do it and whenever you want. Drop out. Leave society as you have known it. Leave it utterly. Blow the mind of every straight person you can reach. Turn them on, if not to drugs, then to beauty, love, honesty, fun."[16]

The postmodern mindset was so easily planted in the American youth psyche at this time because any culture that values conscience-altering experiences (such as LSD trips) is going to have a hard time sticking to an absolute view of life where certain principles are said to always be true no matter what. If you said, "The concrete ground is always hard, no matter what and that is an absolute fact which is always true." The person on LSD might reply, "That's not always the case, when I'm *high* on acid the ground is softer than the air in between these two trees." Now that may not make much sense to you and there might not even be two trees around at the time, but they will claim they have been to a *higher* level of consciousness. Because they *get high*, they see things...feel things, they "*know*" things.

But like postmodernism, there seems to be no distinction between higher and lower levels of consciousness; no up or down, no right or wrong. In a PBS documentary on the hippies, first hand witness Joel Selvin looked back at the purpose of the drug, "The LSD use was a fundamental building block in a new way of thinking in a new community."[15] But what kind of new thinking did the drug ignite? Mary Kasper explains:

> "We really thought that drugs were going to change the world. We really did. We thought if you turned on, if you took acid, you would really change, because we had changed from those experiences. Experiences of cosmic oneness, where I truly felt I was no different than you, I was no different than my black friends; I was no different than anyone who lived in any other part of the world, nor was I that different from my dog." [17]

Once again we see the lack of any qualifying values or absolutes; a dog, a tree, a black person, a white person...it's all the same. Is this good or bad? It's kind of both and yet neither. This is the delirium of postmodernism where life resembles an LSD acid trip.

America's youth movement began with notions of freeing people from having to agree with views they found faulty. But coupled with the idleness of the "teenager," it became about freeing people from all of the "have to" chains of society; freeing one's mind from the matrix of the "musts" in life. "I must...believe this." "I must...stay in line." "I must...go to college." "I must...fit in." "I must...stay in *my* place." "I must... wait my turn." I must...get a job." It is hard to imagine the youth who worked in factories and fields for 16 hours a day at age ten becoming hippies in their teenaged years. But it was not those youth who tuned out; it was the children of the 40s and 50s, the first batch of "teenagers" who grew up with no occupation.

Even today, teens can avoid becoming teenagers. Some young people start charities and raise hundreds of thousands of dollars for those in need. Others start businesses and make more money in their teens then most people will make in their lives. Ephraim Taylor grew up, a young African American boy from St. Louis, who avoided teenagerism. At age twelve he begged his mother for a video game she could not afford to buy. Ephraim found a library book on making video games and stayed after school, after basketball practice to learn the skill. He made his first video game and sold it for $10. He used the profits to start other ventures and made $1 million before graduating from high school.

"Teenagers" on the other hand do not look to become productive until society forces them to at age eighteen or twenty-one or even later. And as America would find out in the 1960s – the definition of the weak noun "teenager" - *ability with no responsibility* is a dangerous combination.

Getting the Big Picture

1. If the term "teenager" is defined as "ability with no responsibility," are/were you a "teenager"?

2. If/when you have children will you allow them to be/become "teenagers"? Why or why not?

3. List some of the abilities that teens possess as well as an appropriate responsibility to go along with each ability.

4. What is the motto of postmodernism? Do you live by this motto?

5. According to the author, why was postmodernism so readily accepted by young adults in the 60s and 70s?

7 A New Family Tree

With the seeds of postmodernism and teenagerism planted in the soil of the 60s, the conditions were ripe for growing a very strange kind of fruit. California Governor Ronald Reagan and San Francisco Mayor Jack Shelley both had run-ins with the "flower children" of the 60s. When the hippies announced to the city that they were planning an enormous gathering of over 100,000 youth in the summer of 1967, Mayor Shelley announced that he would shut down any activity that imposed the hippie happenings on unwilling neighborhoods. Steven Levine immediately objected, "This is really very insidious what he's up to; he wants to stop human growth. He's trying to throw the seeds of this growth out of the sandbox."[1] It is strange that Levine spoke of planting the hippie "seeds of growth" in a sandbox instead of soil. These sand-sown seeds changed America, producing most notably the Sexual Revolution and the 1967 Summer of Love.

Free Love Anyone?

The hippie movement is known for its catch phrase, "Peace & Love." For the "peace" part of it, they are remembered for their demonstrations and protests during the Vietnam War and for marching alongside civil-rights leaders. Standing up to authorities and against racism were prime examples of a growing youth culture that rejected the principles of their parent's generation. But aside from peace they are remembered just as much, if not more, for the "love" portion of their slogan. Not just love, but "free love." This was the epitome of "ability without responsibility." Free love is synonymous with today's sexual practice of NSA (no strings attached) relationships. In the summer of 1967 over 100,000 youth converged on San

Francisco's Haight-Ashbury neighborhood to experience the hippie phenomenon which revolved around a spirit of good will, equality, peace, rock music, communal living, free psychedelic drugs and "free love." Summer of Love participant Phil Morningstar recalled the experience after being drawn to San Francisco by an ad:

> I was looking at all that stuff and they're talking about crash pads, free food, and my father was very intolerant of any views that disagreed with him. So, at fourteen, I took a walk down to the Greyhound bus station, bought a bus ticket; next stop... San Francisco.

> I kind of went crazy when I went there. You could go in Golden Gate Park and sit up on Hippie Hill and meet a group of people, say hi, and just start smoking with them and the next thing... you're at their place, partying with them, and you're sleeping with one of the girls. It was great![2]

This marked the dawn of a brand new freedom in America. But this idea of free love was not brand new. The history of the free love movement can be traced back far before the 1960s and even beyond the borders of America. Europe heard these counter cultural rumblings as early as the 1700s when free love was discussed among small pockets of people, partly as a conversation about women's rights. Women at that time felt oppressed by the way men viewed marriage as giving them possessive rights over their wives but not vice-versa. An important concept to the free love movement was a woman's rights to contraceptives, since raising children was seen as a chief reason why women could not pursue goals in life outside of the home. There were three groups of people who advocated for free love: women in the earliest stages of the feminist movement, homosexuals and anarchists.

Anarchists arose after the Enlightenment Period as antipolitical nonconformists. In fact, everywhere the Enlightenment went, some form of social, political and even religious anarchy followed. Have you ever thought, "Who needs governments telling us what we can and can't do? People should be left to govern themselves without laws and police. You can't trust those people anyway." If so, then you might be interested in the ideas of an anarchist. But, if there were no laws, no police and no leaders, do you imagine that our society would be more or less peaceful? Could you trust people to do what is right? Would people even be able to agree on what is right? What would anarchy – literally 'no order' – look like?

Timing Is Everything

Most people believed that if there was no order, society would not last very long. But at the very least, people did share one thing with the anarchists – a general desire for freedom from being micro-managed by government. One of the ways the anarchists sought to show contempt for "the powers that be" was to challenge areas where they felt the government should have no say. 'Personal relationships' was one such area and marriage was seen by anarchists as just another form of control. Both anarchists and feminists looked at the marriage bond as governmental bondage, while homosexuals resented government for keeping them outside the bounds of marriage. They each saw free love as an alternative. Originally, free love was not about NSA, it was more like NSSA, "No *State* Strings Attached." They were saying, "Don't tell me that I have to get married to my partner, or who I can and can't marry." But it soon took on a more broad meaning as evident in an 1871 speech by Victoria Woodhull, the first woman to run for president of the United States:

> "Yes, I am a Free Lover. I have an inalienable, constitutional and natural right to love whom I may, to love as long or as short a period as I can; to change that love every day if I please, and with that right neither you nor any law you can frame have any right to interfere. [3]

Another pioneering English feminist, Mary Wollstonecraft, refused to marry her lover Gilbert Imlay, even after bearing his child. The relationship came to a painful end when he chose to leave and love another. Mary still continued to promote free love and later, found romance with the English anarchist William Godwin, a staunch advocate for free love. But amazingly, this couple - an anarchist and a feminist, decided to marry just days before her death. Apparently it was not the principle of marriage these individuals rejected; rather, it was the people pushing the principle with whom they had a problem; it was the idea of authority.

In the early twentieth century Japan experienced a free love emergence, slightly different from the above examples. A double standard law "allowed male extramarital sex, but outlawed female infidelity. Japanese free lovers argued that males and females should receive one standard legal treatment....If men can have extramarital sex, so can women, and if women cannot, then neither can men.[4]

The European, anarchist version of free love was handed down and lived out in the bohemian communities of Germany. It was these communities that smuggled the free love ethic into America as the bohemian ideals fueled the worldview of the beatniks, who in turn passed the torch to the hippies. Interestingly, anarchists and homosexuals along with the earlier waves of the feminist movement, all sought to ride the backs of blacks to the ballot in order to help push their own cause forward; cloaking their fight for free love-justice under the rights of blacks by comparing their struggle and oppression to that of "the Negro." But before the 1960s, the free love movement never received anything more than a suspect eye's acknowledgment.

It just so happen that in the 1960s, the stage was set for serious social change. African Americans were making bold stands for civil rights; the country's first batch of idle "teenagers" were becoming young adults; LSD, postmodernism and relativism were being fed to young minds; mistrust had grown among young people towards the values of their parent's; the future was utterly uncertain with scores of young men being drafted to fight in the Vietnam War and the threat of nuclear fallout from the Cold War with Russia; on top of all of that, inspirational leaders like Martin Luther King and JFK were being violently opposed and assassinated – under all this social pressure and anxiety, the moral levies of America broke. And when they broke the waves of free love swept across the country in Katrina-esque fashion. Women were suddenly sexually free; homosexual individuals were not as free, but freer than they had been in times past.[5] After the Summer of Love, San Francisco became a modern "Mecca" for a new type of morality, and America would never be the same.

Between Hippies & Hip Hop

While these changes were taking place among young people in white America, black America was largely caught up in a tug-of-war with the 1960s version of the North vs. South debate in the fight for civil rights. There were some similarities and a few striking contrasts between black youth and the budding hippie counter-culture. For one, hippies had come to distrust authority figures as well as the ideology and religion of their parents and politicians. Likewise, the Hip Hop generation waiting in the wings of the 70s had already learned not to trust the powers that be. For them, police were problematic, and politicians were pathological liars. Distrusting parents was not as much of an issue for young blacks. However, waiting around for their parents' solution to social injustice was not an option for the budding inner-city seedlings. This impatience produced a point of departure from parents on the issue of religion as black youth looked to see who would answer their parent's prayers first, mama and Martin's Jesus, or Malcolm and Muhammad's Allah.

One interesting point of contrast is that hippies outwardly rejected the consumerism and job markets their parents thought so highly of. In the 50s and 60s America experienced a time of prosperity after coming through the Great Depression. Many Americans could not wait to enjoy and exhibit the material wealth of the new economy. This led to what sociologists call "conspicuous consumption;" i.e. showing off your wealth (or worth) by the things you buy. The term, "keeping up with the Jones'" comes from this era. The Jones' represents the classic case of not wanting to be outdone by the next door neighbor. If Mr. Jones has a big new car parked in the driveway today, then tomorrow morning you'll have to trade in your old car and put a bigger new car in your driveway, because you must, "keep up with the Jones'."

The hippies saw this as pretentious and demeaning. How could someone's worth be determined by their possessions? They rejected this and even began to despise money. The Diggers, a community based group of anarchists, known for their theatrics, demonstrated the hippie disgust for money by staging a mock funeral for the "Death of Money." "People dressed in animal heads took money, huge pieces of stage money, and put them in and out of an enormous coffin in a march down Haight Street."[6]

In contrast, the budding black youth movement that would become Hip Hop did not share the hippie's distaste for wealth. Young blacks saw conspicuous consumption as symbolic of success; visual motivation to rise from poverty and struggling to a life of financial security. This made a lasting impression on urban America which can still be seen today from any cursory glance at Hip Hop. Forty years later rappers are still obsessed with brand names and putting on their "shine" (jewelry) to signify their worth. Rapper 50 Cent models this in his song *Poor Lil Rich* where he explains how he lets his watch, car and earring "talk" for him. Because, as he says, "I was a poor nigga, now I'm a rich nigga."

It is unfortunate that 50 did not feel the wealth of his personal worth until he had amassed millions of dollars. But that mindset was modeled in the dominant class of society during the formative years of Hip Hop. And even though the means of attaining success would be different for Hip Hoppers, the end goal was the same. Therefore, the major difference between hippies and Hip Hop can be summed up by Robert Merton's 1957 Strain Theory of cultural change. According to Merton, Hip Hop is mostly "innovative" – because it accepts society's *goals* but rejects (or has been rejected by) the *means* to those goals. Whereas the hippies were "rebels" – rejecting both: society's goals and means.[7]

But there is a counter-culture within each of these cultures. The conscious rapper can be seen as a true "rebel" in Hip Hop because he rejects both commercial America's goals and the means to those goals, refusing to sell out to capitalism. Hippies also have a counter culture within, one that changed from being "rebel" to become "innovative." This innovative group accepted America's materialism as a goal, but found a different means to that goal. This is seen in the fascinating phenomenon that grew into a popular division of American Christianity. In the 70s, Calvary Chapel pastor Chuck Smith, was among a handful of pastors who opened their church's doors to hippies. Soon, a movement was underway known as the Jesus People movement where many hippies came to a life of faith in Jesus Christ. Early on though, a problem arose when many hippie-turned-Christians still held to their personal disdain for employment in America's capitalistic system.

In an attempt to bridge the gap between the hippie's negative attitude towards work and their new faith in God, some pastors began to preach that God would honor the faith of believers by providing for them supernaturally. All they needed to do was believe and through faith they would see miraculous provision and material blessing. The pastors who preached this began to look for scriptural justification for their message, and some found it. This became known as the "prosperity gospel" or the gospel of health and wealth. Many evangelical preachers and bible teachers would soon say that those who preached this message were knowingly or unknowingly taking bible verses out of context to support their claims. If this is true, it would explain why the prosperity gospel only sprang up in writing and preaching from the 1970s onwards.

Connecting the Dots

In 1938, adults traded the Great Depression's idleness for their children's jobs. Two decades of growing up with this idleness produced the hippies – the epitome of ability with no responsibility. But when these white young adults failed to outgrow the addictive "teenager" lifestyle, it had a bizarre effect on the psychological development of black youth. This is because even though white youth have traditionally looked to black art and culture for standards of "cool" in America; still, whites have traditionally set the standards for morality since they have been freer longer to practice the religion of their choice and religion is one of the strongest sources of morality. When white young adults lowered the moral standards for themselves with the Sexual Revolution, free love and a nonchalant attitude toward employment, they unwittingly licensed and validated a mindset that blacks had been trying to erase from their collective consciousness for years. And here's why:

"The [Great] Depression didn't have the impact on Negroes that it had on whites...[since] Negroes had been in the Depression all the time."[8] The "teenager's" separation of ability from responsibility was not new to blacks. During the days of slavery black men felt the responsibility to provide for and protect their families but were robbed of the ability to do so. This produced in many black men the "teenager's" sense of helplessness. Further separation of ability from responsibility came as slaves got wise to the system. "Slaves constructed masks [of] loyalty and laziness to play to their owners fantasies while securing material benefits [for themselves, such as] more food and movement, less work and control."[9] Acting lazy or unable in certain cases actually worked and got the slaves responsibilities reduced. But, after slavery ended, dropping the mask of laziness was difficult because "for many freedmen, emancipation signaled a well deserved vacation...[it seems] the connection between slavery and labor was so intimate that freedom literally meant idleness."[10]

Though African Americans have come a long way, dropping that mask is still hard. Ability with no responsibility is addictive. But the effects are the same for both hippies and Hip Hop. No matter how one comes to accept "teenagerism," the longer they embrace it, the more they are kept, or keep themselves from the job market and free up jobs for someone else just as the 1938 law was intended to do. White youth, who either could not or would not return to their parents for jobs, money or help with education after the hippie years, felt the negative impact of the "teenager" syndrome on their adult lives. Also, when inner city youth embrace the ethic of the "teenager," they waste years that could be spent preparing for their future.

Now, instead of living up to the social standards of whites, black youth have had the culturally confusing option and excuse of living down to white standards as well. In 2009, rappers

Gucci Mane and Plies demonstrated how young blacks reject white "coolness" even while they reflect white moral standards. In the song *Wasted*, they proclaim, "I'm no hippie, but I'm stoned...I don't wear tight jeans like the white boys...but I do get wasted like the boys." They imply, "It's okay for us to do it, because they do it."

This is one reason why some have criticized the pursuit of equality between blacks and whites, questioning whether that should be the goal. In *The State of Black America 2007*, forwarded by the then Senator Barak Obama, the authors continually compare the statistical progress of black Americans to that of whites in areas such as education, and political involvement. The aim seems to be for blacks to catch up to where whites currently are; not just having equal opportunities, but equal outcomes. But what if the place where whites are is not a good place at all? Should blacks or any other group settle for equality with a leading group who has begun to settle?

Happily Never After

The "teenager" concept is a bad seed. If we do not see the connection between the seed and the fruit, we will continue to plant the suspect seeds and be doomed to reap the horrible harvest. The most rancid fruit of the "teenager" is the destruction of the American family.

There are two legal landmarks that helped to establish turning points in American family life: one is the Family Act of 1969 and the other, the 1973 case of Roe v. Wade, which won for women the right to an abortion on demand. These laws were not brand new considerations solely in light of the hippie youth movement. But, with the events of the 60s, society had prepared itself for a moral shift that would not have occurred in America before these "teenagers" became voters.

How did it begin? Much of the credit for starting the moral shift goes to the 1959 Casey Report which shocked the country concerning the level of marital infidelity, homosexual thought or activity and pedophilia Americans admitted to. Many have since questioned the methods and merit of Casey's study, nonetheless, once the results were published, Americans began to wonder if average people still held to the traditional values of marriage and family. But even if some Americans were no longer holding those values, it is clear that those values were holding America together.

Marriage was the first to go. Before 1969, if there was unhappiness in a marriage, divorce was not easy to come by. In fact, one or both of the spouses needed to prove just cause for a divorce; such as marital unfaithfulness or cruelty. Sometimes, however, they resorted to what lawyers called "legal fiction" where couples would cooperate in a lie in order to convince the judge to grant them a divorce.

In an attempt to protect the seriousness and sincerity of the oath taken in a court of law (to tell the truth, the whole truth and nothing but), lawyers and judges sought to relieve unhappily married couples from the pressure of lying just to get a divorce. To achieve this California passed the Family Act of 1969, that beginning January 1, 1970, either party in a marriage could obtain a divorce from the other without having to prove fault, even if the other party did not want the divorce. This became known as the No Fault Divorce law. Consider the irony – in an attempt to keep couples from lying under oath to get a divorce, the solution was to allow them to turn a different oath into a lie – the one made during their wedding vowing to be together, "til death do us part."

There were warnings that this would have a devastating impact on the nation. Arnold J. Gibbs, the chairman of the American Bar Association's Family Law Section, warned that,

"The creation of a mere 'rubber stamp type' of divorce procedure would not be in the best interests of the family, its individual members, and society in general."[12] This warning was not heeded. Other states soon followed California's lead, turning spouses who made wedding vows into potential victims at the whim of their partner. Roughly eighty-percent of the divorces in America are now one-sided, not joint decisions.[13] The divorced spouse is not the only victim however, as Maggie Gallagher points out in her book, *The Abolition of Marriage*. The fact that we changed from a marriage culture to a divorce culture is "the driving force behind almost all of the gravest problems facing America - crime, poverty, welfare dependence, homelessness, educational stagnation, even child abuse."[14]

Look at the statistics for these social ills and you will see a drastic climb up the charts from the 1960s to the present. The doing away with marriage strikes children with poverty, or at least puts them in a poorer state than they would have been had their parents been married and stayed married. The statistics tell the story of the change in the culture after the No Fault Divorce law. For instance, just fourteen-percent of white women who married in the 1940s eventually divorced by the 1990s. But of those who married only a single generation later in the late 1960s and early 1970s, almost fifty-percent had divorced by the mid 1990s.[15] And though blacks were once more likely to marry than whites, with family remaining strong and intact from the time of slavery at least until the Great Depression, since then the black family has drastically declined with whites following along the same lines.[16, 17]

The free love movement, mixed with the free "teenager" movement changed the social landscape of America by changing what we call 'love, marriage and family' to what Ciara and Justin Timberlake called *Love, Sex and Magic*. Sex is no longer the bodily mirror of marriage vows and the way to bring children into a committed family. Instead, it is seen only as a magical, mystical encounter. But if sex could be just that, there would not be anything like the kind of social decay we are witnessing today where an estimated 24 million American children are growing up with absent fathers, and a high percentage of them are African-American."[18] In 2008, CNN reported on a study which claimed that the United States spends $112 billion of tax payer money per year on children of single parents in the areas of welfare, healthcare, and the judicial system, since children of single parents are more likely to have run-ins with law enforcement.[19]

This is possibly why "old heads" in the community used to help foster a sense of shame whenever someone turned up pregnant outside of marriage. They knew the impact it would have on society if unmarried moms became the norm. Our cities' epidemic of criminally minded youth stems directly from fatherlessness. But marriage is what ties fathers to homes; remove marriage on a massive scale and you will invite chaos. Gallagher warns, "When one couple divorces, the chance their son will become a juvenile delinquent may be quite low. But when a whole community adopts the pattern, everyone's sons and daughters are at risk."[20] This shows the tremendous weight that marriage carries. Sadly, since the dawn of free love we don't see sex as being as big of a deal as marriage; we have separated the two and have failed to ask ourselves if we like the results. Instead, we bury our conscience along with any evidence of wrong doing.

In true "teenager" fashion, the late 60's and 70's was a time when people began to run from responsibility in all its forms; running from spouses and even from children. But for women in particular, running from children was difficult; that is, before 1973. In the landmark case of Roe v. Wade, it was ruled that a woman has the right to receive an abortion on demand because the baby is in "her body." This was based on the Constitutional "right to privacy" which can be gleaned from the

Fourteenth Amendment. Once again, the "teenager" was struggling to match ability with responsibility; freedom and consequence. Norma L. McCorvey, aka Jane Roe, claimed she had been raped but later confessed that this was a lie and that she had really become pregnant due to failed contraceptives. None the less, the case helped women win this right and over time other laws were passed to help structure or strengthen abortion laws.

But abortion is not an easy way out. A 2009 article published in Current Woman's Heath Review found that abortion has greater impact on future parenting than other forms of pregnancy loss and that "emotional responses after induced abortion are more likely to go unresolved and to persist for a longer time period....With 20-30 percent" of the "1.3 million U.S. abortions performed annually, a minimum of 130,000 new cases of abortion-related mental health problems appear each year."[21] Even without abortion, America has an embarrassingly high infant mortality rate. Shockingly, there is even a link between the decline of marriage and the high death rate of newborn babies, says Nicholas Eberstadt of the Harvard Center for Population and Development Studies.[22] Interestingly, in 1995, Norma McCorvey changed her views on abortion, quit her job at a Dallas woman's clinic and joined ranks with the pro-life movement.[23]

The Assisted Suicide of the Family

The forces fighting against the family have been at work for many years. In the 1920's, Margaret Sanger founded the organization which eventually became Planned Parenthood, specializing in birth control measures. Sanger taught negative eugenics, which involves keeping or discouraging people who are considered mentally, physically or socially "unfit" from reproducing. Some charge that her programs were aimed specifically at African Americans to reduce the black population, but research suggests that many blacks just so happened to fall into her true targeted population – the poor. She traveled to Europe, Asia and Africa and even spoke to the Ku Klux Klan with her message of birth control as a means to reduce the population and keep children from being born into disadvantageous circumstances.

Sanger's ultimate desire was to liberate working white women whom she saw as being used as "human incubators." She taught that families should be educated about the "higher standard of living they could enjoy without children, and that couples should note how much more enjoyable the sex act is when performed without the fear of child bearing."[24] Though she advocated birth control she was not at all in favor of abortion, though her organization later became one of the top providers of the procedure. Sanger can be considered a "free lover" since, even though she married twice, "she had a number of well publicized affairs with prominent men, including Havelock Ellis and H.G. Wells."[25] It was Havelock Ellis, one of her greatest mentors, who taught that the poor should be mandatorily sterilized.

W.E.B. Du Bois objected to scientific racism and eugenics, yet he participated in Margaret Sanger's *Birth Control Review* in 1932, admitting that, "The more intelligent class [of blacks] uses birth control....[while] the mass of ignorant Negroes still breed carelessly and disastrously, so that the increase among Negroes, even more than the increase among whites, is from that part of the population least intelligent and fit, and least able to rear their children properly."[26] This was not said out of a race based self-hatred, but was based on his view that a "talented tenth" of the Nation's blacks should be highlighted to lead the way for the rest.

In giving a creed for youth to follow in 1946, Du Bois encouraged "marriage by careful planning [and] children limited by thoughtful foresight."[27] He obviously had no intention of supporting the idea of birth control for the purpose of free love, but by teaming with Sanger, he lent steam to her agenda in the black community. The Abstinence Clearing House sees that her agenda was about more than just free love. Over the last ninety years, they believe, the values of Margaret Sanger's organization have become the "values of western civilization." But her message "promised more liberties to a minority [at the top] at the expense of a pacified majority [at the bottom], whose compliance was to be purchased by giving them unlimited sexual gratification without the burden of the resulting children."[28]

We have discussed how Hip Hop has been commercialized so that it is no longer an adjective, but a noun...a thing to be marketed. "Teenager" has also become a noun; a thing to be marketed to. American businesses lost their young, cheap labor in 1938, but later found that they had another way to exploit youth. Idle teens have become the most money spending demographic in America. Teens went from producers to purchasers, from contributors to consumers. But retailers have accelerated the purchasing appetite of teens by transforming yet another "how" into a "what" – Sex. Ideally, sex is not a "thing," but a "way." It is the "way" that married couples physically reflect their vows and bring children into a committed family. But sex has become a thing to be marketed along with other commercial products. Movies, music and made-for-TV shows target youth and constantly bump up the sexual content in order to ensure commercial sponsors that money yielding youth will be watching.[29]

In the book *Teenage*, Jon Savage sees that Europe has been dealing with teen culture since the late 1800s, much longer than we have in America. In that teen filled land, during the 1940s, Christian author C.S. Lewis, who penned the Chronicles of Narnia, warned his non-Christian audience that "there are people who want to keep our sex instinct inflamed in order to make money out of us. Because" he says, "a man with an obsession is a man who has very little sales resistance."[30] Culture, youth and intimacy have all been commercialized and sold back to us at a price we cannot afford; buying into this has morally bankrupted our society. We have examined the historical seed and the soil of what was sown in the 60s. We can return to the present to see how this strange fruit has impacted and stunted the growth of manhood and womanhood in America, but specifically in the urban arena.

Getting the Big Picture

1. If the Summer of Love had never occurred, what do you suppose family life in America would be like today?

2. If the Summer of Love had not yet occurred in American history, but was scheduled to occur next summer in your city, would you support this event? Would you attend? Why or why not? What would you say to others thinking of attending?

3. Name two things that Hip Hop has in common with the hippies.

4. How do the hippies and Hip Hop differ?

8 The Grown-boy Syndrome

Our culture is obsessed with youth. Medical breakthroughs allow us to live longer lives while we invest countless time and money into looking and feeling younger. But our anti-aging society has insisted on living younger too. Not just moving at the energetic, untiring pace of youth; but living with the empty, unwise pursuits of youth. A passage in the Bible tells readers to "flee youthful lusts." These "lusts" are not called youthful because they are okay for youth to have, but because it is understandable that youth would have them since many do not yet know how to desire anything more than what their five senses suggest. They have not yet developed an appetite or appreciation for that which is most nutritious and nourishing. They prefer a piece of candy over a piece of cantaloupe and a night of fiesta over a night with the family. The age at which this youthfulness ends varies around the world; however in America we are given endless time to pursue "youthful lusts."

The Man-child in the Media

Consider the role of some of the leading "men" in today's media. Often they are the roles of a man-child; the *age* of manhood, but stuck in the *stage* of boyhood. Comedic actors Jim Carrey, Adam Sandler and Will Farrell have made their careers off of mirroring for us the culture's uncultivated males. Our sitcoms are full of them, our movies, our malls, our families, our penitentiaries, our parliament; they pop up everywhere.

In 2008 Brad Pitt portrayed the epitome of a man-child in *The Curious Case of Benjamin Button*. Benjamin was mysteriously born as an infant with an old-aged body. Throughout the course of his life his body grew younger as he chronologically got older. It was thrilling to see a person aging in reverse until the drama of the story began to unfold. Benjamin's growth problem began to complicate his love life. Technically he was getting older, but at the same time, in a very disruptive and disturbing way, he was also growing too young to do the things a man should.

After fathering a child with his leading lady, he decided it would be best for him to leave them since he could not possibly take care of a child in his reverse-aging condition. Ultimately, Benjamin was unable to carry on any relationship with his beloved other than one of complete dependence. He ended up in her arms, a helpless grown-boy, being taken care of by the woman in his life. Sadly, this fits the description of too many males in our society. When applied to Hip Hop, it is all too obvious that we are suffering from our own curious case of the Grown-boy Syndrome.

Jay Z's Blueprint for Manhood

In the late 1980s there was a popular TV show called *Thirty Something*. A young child watching that show would have been confused by the way these thirty-something year olds had more money and freedom, and yet their love lives were somehow just as messy as many "teenagers'." But it actually made sense. If someone was "thirty-something" in the late 80's, then they would have been a teen during the 60's. The show revealed the long-term effects from the cultural changes of the Sexual Revolution and the Summer of Love.

The theme song for *Thirty Something* might just as well have been Jay Z's 2006 comeback track by the same name in which he proclaimed, "*30's the new 20.*" The idea behind the song was that the mature age of thirty-something was now just as cool as it once was to be twenty-something. Mature listeners liked the idea of the song, but there were three instant problems: First, when the song released, some radio hosts and every Jay Z "hater" instantly pointed out that Jay only had about two years left to be thirty-anything.

The second problem was the proof given to validate Jay's maturity. In the first line he talked about still being "hot," having the best looking girl, a better car, and starting trends. These did not cause teens to think more "grown up" thoughts than what they were already thinking. During a 2009 interview, Jay Z claimed, "I cannot relate to a 15 year old. I deal with mature and relevant topics for my age group."[1] But on this "grown-up" song, the only difference between being thirty-something and twenty-something was biological age. The song ended up highlighting the very thing it was meant to hide, and rather than communicating "I've matured with age," one could argue that the song was really an attempt to say, "I still wish I was," "I still think I am," *or* "I still am...young."

Lastly, most current rap stars had already cemented their claim to the children and maybe even to childhood by making the words "lil" (little) or "young" a permanent part of their moniker. In mid 2009, mature rappers Master Ace and Ed OG released the song *Little Young* in which they named every rapper who has ever had the words "little" or "young" as part of their name. This was their way of frowning on the idea that Hip Hop is only a sport to be played by the man-child. They did not name Jay Z among the young-stars, perhaps because Jay has made valiant efforts to mature in the eyes of the culture. And yet one of his nick-names throughout his career has been "Young" or "Young Hova" derived from yet another one of his self inflicted nick-names, "the god MC – J-hova."

On his *Blueprint 3* album, the "god" tries to flash his maturity by flaunting his "O"-nipotence – his ties with Oprah and Obama. He talks about putting the guns away, and no longer rapping about selling crack, only to turn around and potentially "offend [his] political connects" on *DOA* where he encourages young listeners to "get violent" and "commit felonies." He closed the album with the song *Forever Young* where he imagines the legend of his name "Young" and hopes to get "younger every year" as his story is retold. He says it's like "living life in rewind."

Unlike other forms of music, Hip Hop artists are not allowed to grow up. This is why younger artists who dis Jay Z attack his age. Due to the massive fatherlessness in the African American community, young blacks are not used to receiving authoritative words from older black men. This is the struggle artists like Jay Z will face unless something changes. Jay would have probably done a greater service for youth and better represented the mature had he flossed a new value system for a culture in massive moral need. But for several reasons (discussed in chapter 10) he could not do this.

Though recently married, Jay never mentioned that fact on the album but did however brag that his "hoe [is] so sick;" which perhaps, is a compliment to whoever he is referring to as his "hoe." Jay Z's rival Joe Budden hinted at the problem in the 10 minute tirade *Who Killed Hip Hop*. He asked listeners, "Do we just think yall gettin' dumber/ by tryin' to make gettin' older gettin' younger/ As our jeans got tighter and our shirts got longer/ we're tryin to figure out which age group that we belong to." Growing in fashion and trends has not produced an adult generation of Hip Hop.

Jay Z's lack of clarity on the issue of maturity has even led to scandal. The song *On to the Next One* was supposed to showcase Jay Z as always beyond the plateau of his peers. While they are on what's "now," he is on what's "next." But being unwilling or unwitting of how to show what "next" looks like, Jay was left so clueless when the time came to film the video that he agreed to the most bizarre concept for the shoot. So bizarre was the video that a YouTube activist known as the "the

Forerunner," got the online world in an uproar with what he called "hardcore research" linking Jay Z to the anarchist movement known as the Free Masons and devil worship.

In *The Jay Z Deception* the Forerunner's "research" was mainly suspicion, fiction and creative imagination linked to a few historical facts. But he was right about one thing. In the attempt to get out from under all authority, history's anarchist movements have undermined marriage – the basis for family, and turned men and women into the most unfitting candidates for parenthood. If this goes unchecked, it will defeat the human race.

Even without the elaborate efforts taken by the Forerunner to connect rappers to the Free Masons, the culture can still be found guilty of spreading anarchy. A quack doctor can wrongly diagnose a real HIV patient with imaginary illnesses using absurd evidence, and still be right about the fact that the patient is dying from HIV. In diagnosing Hip Hop, this is how history may remember the Forerunner. But make no mistake; the Grown-boy Syndrome is spreading, and approaching epidemic levels.

Symptoms of the Syndrome

Sadly, many young males growing up in society have only the man-child model of manhood to pattern themselves after. Most young men with absent fathers swear they will be nothing like their dads when they grow up. Yet the men they look up to and get their "swagger" from are more like their fathers than they care to admit. The "man-child" in the media only appears to be better than the average deadbeat dad because of his money and visibility. These are often mistaken for manhood because they are the two things deadbeat dads fail to provide.

When talking to teens in the classroom, upon mentioning the word 'father' a strange phenomenon occurs. The eyes roll and a gust of wind hurls through the room as if thirty bandages were suddenly ripped from thirty broken hearts, releasing pounds of pressure which exits the body like hot steam through the windpipes. The class simultaneously lets out a sigh of frustration. Pssssss!!!!!! They have nothing good to say about fathers. But many males are left limping down the same path, lengthening their father's lackluster legacy. This is not just the sigh of the common; even the celebrity sings this sad song. In 2009, just as Lil Wayne prepared to head to the award show to see about his eight Grammy nominations, he sat down for a telling interview with Katie Kouric. Katie asked:

"How'd you get the name Lil Wayne…Your real name is Dwayne right, so why'd you drop the D?"

Lil Wayne responded sincerely, "I'll tell you right here on T.V. I dropped the D, because I'm a junior. My father's living, and he's not in my life. And he's never been in my life. So I don't wanna be Dwayne, I'd rather be Wayne."[2]

It would be nice to see Wayne, in his attempt to repudiate his father's legacy, choose a role model who treats women with respect and is the complete opposite of his father. Ironically, Lil Wayne pledges his allegiance to, has a Father-Son relationship with and has even recorded an album entitled *Like Father Like Son* with the artist "Baby," and Wayne himself already has at least four children by four different women.

In the opening scene of rapper 50 Cent's semi-autobiographical movie, *Get Rich or Die Trying*, Curtis Jackson tells us that throughout his life he was on a search to find one important person, his father. After taking us through the ups and downs of inner-city living, the last words of the movie are sobering and sad: "I spent all this time looking for my father, only to realize that I was really looking for myself." This reveals a default state of mind that many young males slip into. Having played the role of father in their own lives for so long, they come to believe that they didn't really need dad the way they once thought. But this is not true.

Even if young males don't look to their own fathers, they make up composite sketches of foster father figures. They may take one man's bravado; and another man's hustle; and yet another's approach to women; and still, another's man's nickname and glory, as was the case with Curtis Jackson who admired the New York gangster, 50 Cent. Young males will find a father figure for their family portrait, even if the foster father has to be formed from fragmented photos of fact and fiction and forced into the frame. Mothers, wives, girlfriends and children are then forced to live with the various personas that young men take on in place of their dads.

Wayne and 50 are not the only rappers who've reported the impact of fatherlessness in their lives. Detroit rapper, Elzhi from the group Slum Village leaks his emotion on *The Leak*:

> Few years before that...my pops wiped his feet for the last time on our doormat/ Look deep in my heart, you'll see where the sore's at

Hip Hop is full of these kinds of examples. To close out the *Rock Lafamilia* album, Jay Z and Beanie Segal unleashed a scathing rebuke of their absentee fathers on the song *Where Have You Been?* Beans, one of the more street strong rappers in the game almost reverts back to childhood in tears of anger and pain as he confronts his father for abusing his mother and leaving his family; for not teaching him how to fight, fix a flat tire or what manhood was about.

In another song, *Meet the Parents*, Jay Z gives one of the most vivid depictions of the Grown-boy Syndrome's impact on inner-city life. He tells the story of a woman named Isis and a "man" named Mike who loved the fast life. Isis soon becomes pregnant but after seeing the baby boy, Mike denies paternity and abandons her. He never sees his son again until one fateful day when father and son are reunited as strangers on the street. Mike notices that the youngster looks a little like him and tells the boy to get off of the street. The father and son are caught up in the tension of the moment and both draw their guns to deal with the perceived threat. The son pauses as he notices how the older "man" looks like a more mature version of himself. But the pause is just enough time for Mike's instinct to kick in as he pulls the trigger, ending the young boy's life. Jay Z ends the saga with the ominous admonition, "Fathers be a father; you're killing your sons."

This was excellent advice, but it was only partial advice. What does it mean to "be a father?" Most young dads have a mental measuring cup into which they pour time and money. In order to judge whether or not they are pouring in enough, they look back at how much their own fathers poured into them. After measuring themselves this way, many feel good about themselves, thinking, "Hey, at least I'm doing more than my father did for me." But just how much is enough?

Happy Donor's Day

In June of 2009, Mary J. Blige's step-daughter Briana put her father on blast by going on-line and tweeting to the virtual world, "Somebody find my father so I can tell him Happy Donor's Day."[3] It is difficult for fathers to be more than just sperm donors without being present; and it is difficult to be present without living in the home. To ease the pressure that non-residential fathers feel about not living with their children, some psychoanalysts assert that just spending daily "quality time" with children should be enough to do the job of parenting. The quality time that a parent spends with their child is about ten to fifteen minutes a day (so they say). And if just ten to fifteen minutes will do it, then there is no reason why a divorced or visiting parent cannot be a good "enough" parent and make up for the lost time.[4]

But even if just fifteen quality minutes a day were enough to be a good parent, what matters is the ability to be around for the right fifteen minute window when it happens. It could be the five minutes in the morning, combined with the two minute conversation after that commercial with the sexually suggestive message, mixed with four minutes of overhearing a conversation between dad and mom during dinner, plus the four minute dialog before bedtime that make up the fifteen impactful parenthood moments. In other words, you cannot choose which fifteen minutes will be impactful, those moments chose you! But they can only do so as dad is present.

David Blankenhorn counsels, "To be a good-enough father – to sustain the dailiness of effective parenting – a man needs to live with his children."[5] Children need ample access to authority and affection. Not simply one or the other. But the loss of marriage in America makes this almost impossible. Maggie Gallagher agrees, "For father[s], in particular, marriage plays a crucial role in attaching them to their children. Marriage creates a unity of interest between them and their children.[6] When Dad is married to Mom and in the home, think of all of the natural connections for him to share with his children – "our family name"..."our reputation"..."our home"...Mom is "our leading lady." But presently, the only things many non-residential fathers and their children share are a sense of distance and the awkwardness of trying to find something positive they have in common. This is not to question the love that modern fathers have for their children, but as Blankenhorn points out, "from the child's perspective, parental love without parental capacity [to show that love] is primarily a reminder of loss."[7]

Didactic Dad

The loss of marriage has led to the loss of manhood and fatherhood. This keeps the self-help ideas of Hip Hop in high demand. To understand why, we must uncover the primal link between Hip Hop and men's role in the family. In the classic old school hit *Ain't No Half Steppin'* Big Daddy Kane rapped, "The name is Big Daddy, you know as in your father, so when you hear a dope rhyme believe that I'm the author." In the new millennium, Jay Z wrote a *Reminder*, comparing his lyrics to "verses permanently tattooed" which "serve as mementoes."

What these artists sensed was the very real connection between literature, leadership and fatherhood. The word "author" is traced back to a Latin word *auctor* which means "increase," "one who causes to grow," "originator" or "father."[8] It eventually came to mean "one who puts things in writing." In a family setting, it is the father's job to set forth the mandates for matters of maturity. Dads lay down the law of how things go as things grow. For this reason, "author" is also where we get our word "augment" which means "to add to, enhance, enlarge or expand."

The same Latin word is where we get the word "authority." It originally meant "book or quotation that settles an argument." If something was written, it had "fatherly" status. Unlike mom, the father has a unique role in a family. Maybe it is because of the bass in his voice, or his stature, but normally, fathers are the only ones who get to speak unilaterally into our lives; unilaterally meaning "one-sided." They speak and we listen, and there is not a lot of back and forth about it. Whether or not fathers abuse this privilege or fail to use it at all is not the point; the point is that this is their role. What they authoritatively say goes unchallenged and unchanged until a person is out of their father's house. Anytime someone attempts to speak into someone else's life in a one-sided arrangement, they are consciously or unconsciously playing the father's role.*

When rappers step into the booth with their writings, they are leading. But when we don't challenge their leading, they move from leader to father (author) or at least father figure. This is why Detroit Holy Hip Hopper, DJ Nobel says, "We should always be mentally (if not verbally) having conversations with our music and media," especially if the artists have very un-father-like things to say.

Body Art?

When dads are absent we seek authoritative answers in the strangest settings and get them in the weirdest ways. Tattoos and body art can actually be seen as an attempt to regain fatherly authority for one's self. A synonym for the ancient Hebrew word "law" is the term "statute" which literally means to "cut into" or "inscribe." When God gave Moses the Law (the 10 Commandments) we are told that his words were "cut into" the side of a mountain. When words are inscribed, or cut into something, they are unchanging. This is why the word "author" was fitting for "fathers." Hebrew fathers were told to bind God's "law" or "inscriptions" to their wrists, foreheads and door posts and teach them to their children.† Even though we don't have many fathers today, we still have our own versions of father-like "inscribing" and "cutting into" things.

When artists record an album, it is referred to as "cutting" a record because sonic or digital information is being cut into wax or burned into a CD. When people get tattoos, needles are literally cutting and inscribing into the skin. In the song *Best to Do It*, Detroit battle/gangsta rapper Royce the 5'9" confesses, "The tattoo had to be in the right spot/ to remind me

---

*Interestingly, in the Bible it is praiseworthy for listeners to test the biblical accuracy of a minister's message. (Acts 17:11)

† The Bible, Deuteronomy 6:1-9

of how notorious that my life got." Some of our most popular athletes and entertainers are covered with tattoos. Some have even hid their entire faces behind writing. Youth and young adults now have an obsession with writing on themselves. Some statement, some slogan, some name, some image, something must be inscribed to tell me (and those who see it) what my life is about. This is an attempt to make up for the loss of a father's authoritative, unquestionable, unchanging inscription in our lives.

When talking with young people, one finds that those with strong fathers in their lives might get a tattoo for fashion or to fit in, while those without strong fathers, somehow feel as though they *need* tattoos and must have them. There is another, not so artistic, version of cutting that happens perhaps for the same reason. Why is it that young people have resorted to cutting and piercing themselves all over in an attempt to deal with their emotional trauma, leaving indelible marks? Could it be an attempt to regain the authority they missed from not having a loving father's lasting laws properly cut into the family stone?

Hey Ma'

A new morality has been developed, one that disconnects fathers from the family. This new morality only sees a responsibility toward children and not to the child's mother. *The Maury Povich Show* helped to popularize the phrase "I take care of my 'responsibilities'" concerning children. But this only serves to strengthen the misguided view that the most important aspect of having a child is the financial obligation. It is then believed that as long as dad contributes financially and is 'available' time-wise, then he is responsible - why care about anything else? This is blatantly stated for fun in the opening lines of 50 Cent's song *Get Money* where he teases that one way to become a millionaire is to have a baby by him. He adds, "I'll write the check before the baby's comes, who the f*** cares?" T.I. comes close to this sentiment in his 2009 release *Be Like That*, where he disses his first "baby's mama," saying "I owe money for my son, honey and nothing more." Ice Cube depicts this theatrically in the film *First Sunday*, telling his "baby's mama," "You're not my responsibility anymore, my son is."

But aside from diapers, clothes and time with dad, one of the major contributions of a father to a child is the modeling aspect of manhood, such as when the youngster gets to grow up watching dad and mom unconditionally love one another through the various stages of life. It is not just enough for a child not to see mommy and daddy fighting, it is just as important for a child to see them loving, sacrificing and solving conflicts. A young male watching this will learn firsthand how to handle one of the biggest subjects facing him in life – women! He will learn that the test of manhood is not having women, but rather how skillful a man is in dealing with one woman. A young woman growing up watching this type of man will learn the difference between a man and a man-child. She will spot the counterfeit a mile away and steer clear of him, saving herself much heartache and headache.

We must get to the point where we do more than challenge young men to be "responsible" about pregnancy and children. Usually all we mean is 'wear a condom' and 'if she gets pregnant, get a job that will cover the expenses' and 'be present enough.' Meanwhile, the way grown-boys deal with females goes unaddressed. This can be seen in the Father's Day appeals of Barack Obama, before and after becoming President. He said:

> *In 2007*: Let's admit to ourselves that there are a lot of men out there that need to stop acting like boys; who need to realize that responsibility does not end at conception; who need to know that what makes you a man is not the ability to have a child but the courage to raise a child.

In 2008: Any fool can have a child. That doesn't make you a father. It's the courage to raise a child that makes you a father.

In 2009: I had a heroic mom and wonderful grandparents who helped raise me and my sister, and it's because of them that I'm able to stand here today....But despite all their extraordinary love and attention, that doesn't mean that I didn't feel my father's absence. That's something that leaves a hole in a child's heart....Just because your own father wasn't there for you, that's not an excuse for you to be absent also. It's all the more reason for you to be present.[9]

But if we believe that a father's presence is the issue, why are we so reluctant to challenge men on the one issue that powerfully deals with this - the relation of sex to marriage? Character and commitment to the marriage vows make it socially safe to procreate and psychologically sane to engage in sex (I mean this to say that it is insane otherwise). On Father's Day 2009, President Obama announced his hopes to spark a "national conversation on responsible fatherhood." But if that conversation is spoken in the language of free love, the talks will break down. To talk of "responsible fathers" without talking about committed husbands misses the point. We will only end up trying to figure out what is "responsible enough" and "how much" dads can still do once they vacate the home, the headquarters from which this privilege and duty is carried out. Gallagher adds that through marriage:

A father shows his children and their mother that he loves them by putting their needs first. His sexuality is (in theory) at his wife's disposal, not other women's – and therefore cannot threaten the well-being of his children. His income is their income. His emotional energy and financial energy are also theirs.[10]

This is responsible fatherhood.

Good Sex like Good Credit

In teaching character education to young adults, my

motto has been, "Sex without marriage is corny; marriage without character is crazy." To illustrate this I turn to the 2007 *video* documentary *Maxed Out*, which exposed the way credit card companies prey on vulnerable segments of society, particularly college students. The documentary observed how credit agencies target youth today, compared to the way these companies conducted business years ago.

They highlight a 1950's black and white commercial where a credit agency lists the three things a person must have in order to be approved for a credit card: Character (trustworthiness – a history of keeping financial commitments), Capacity (the ability to pay bills – a job) and Capital (some type of collateral, such as a savings account or land). Today however, credit card companies target those with the least amount of character, no capacity to pay bills and no collateral whatsoever. College students end up in enormous debt and credit card companies live off the interest and penalties charged to them for years. At long last, in President Obama's first year in office, the government went after these companies for what they called "predatory lending."

This is a perfect picture of what is happening to us socially and morally when it comes to sex and marriage. The ideal used to be that sex was saved for marriage – something for which you needed character (a man had to prove to a young woman and her family that he could be trusted to keep vows), capacity (he had to have a way to provide for a family which was the inevitable result) and capital (of course it helped if he had a little something saved up for a rainy day). Sex without these is like the predatory lending of credit cards to college kids – we end up socially in debt, still paying for our decisions long after they were made.

The Fatherless Generation

In the first chapter we said that a generation can be identified by the shared attitudes and interests that mark a group of people during a specific time in history. Consider this then, from the 1970's all the way up to the present, we are looking at one massive, growth stunted generation which shares the same struggle – broken families. In our nation, families either fail to form, or else they do form, but then break up and then 7000 blended families form every week even though sixty percent of all second marriages fail.[11] This failure and fatherlessness has become the greatest common denominator of the present generation.

In Hip Hop generation 1 (raised in the 70's and 80's) and Hip Hop generation 2 (raised in the 90's and new millennium) we have an interesting phenomenon; for the first time in American history, parents and youth share the exact same culture. Hip Hop generation 1 has their own, "old school" heroes, but they also share the new school heroes with their children. The fact that parents and youth share the same culture is not at all problematic. It is a testimony to the richness and durability of the culture. Through Hip Hop, African Americans have regained a sense of identity that can be passed down to their children. What is troublesome is the fact that parents and youth not only share the same vocabulary, heroes and fashion, but also the same values, habits and future.

The adults have no seasoned wisdom to offer their youth. This stunted moral growth comes from the ingrown, ungrown "teenager" syndrome which produced the man-child in the 60's. Young blacks in Hip Hop are not alone. Listen and you will hear voices from other genres; desperately struggling to survive as they walk along these uncertain shores, surrounded by the sharp shards of shattered family. Pop star Pink deals with this in her song *Family Portrait*, where she portrays her younger self asking her fracturing family if they could go back to "normal" and "happy," no longer having to split the holidays and change last names; telling daddy, "I need you around." In 2009, R&B singer Usher endorsed an eleven year old white youth; the musical prodigy Justin Beiber. One of Justin's first hits, a ballad, asked his absent father, "Where are you now that I'm half grown?"

Detroit rapper Eminem serves as living proof of this cross-cultural calamity. Known for being one of the most successful and talented rappers, white or black, to ever grab the mic; he is also known for heavily decorating his music with the family dysfunction he personally endured, first from his own parents, then with the mother of his daughter whom he married twice and divorced twice. His pain and the search for a solution led him to and keeps him in the media. The media has become the meeting place for this generation's group therapy. In an interview entitled *The Rehabilitation of Eminem*, when asked about his drug addiction and upcoming *Relapse* album, Eminem admitted to asking his musical mentor for advice. Should he reinvent himself artistically as some suggested? Dr. Dre responded, "People want to see you wild the f*** out and lose your mind again."[12] The result was an album full of dysfunctional fun for the whole broken family.

Hip Hop has a more colorful way of expressing what the generation at large is feeling. In his song *My Life*, West Coast rapper The Game bares his emotional pain like one of his many tattoos. He shows that fractured family is the number one struggle of this generation when he talks about how, as a child, he needed his father, but tragically, his father "needed a needle" (a reference to drug addiction). Then with shocking force in the second verse, Game delivers his "(Eric) sermon" to his generation, "F*** Jessie Jackson cuz it ain't about race now." Upon first hearing this, one wonders 'how could someone say such a thing?' Why the verbal flagrant foul against Civil Rights leader Jessie Jackson, the man who was by Dr. King's side at his assassination? But then the declaration that the struggle is no longer about race strikes a sobering chord.

Race does not matter the way it once did. As technology expands the world has culturally shrunk and the divisions have dissolved. A New York Times article entitled *Generation E.A.: Ethnically Ambiguous* stated that this generation is more attracted to marketing models whose racial background is hard to pin down. Blond-haired, blue-eyed models are working less and less.[13] This diverse generation does not necessarily know or care how they got the rights to vote, move, ride and learn wherever they please. For many of them history is not real, just as math is not relevant. It is not struggles of racial equality that concerns them. It is the struggle to produce something other than the dysfunction they've seen growing up in communities full of broken families, even while the media and every earthly influence pushes them toward the same selfish agendas that took away one or both of their parents. This struggle unites rich and poor, black and white. Help them over this hurdle and you will have succeeded at taking the thorn out of the lion's paw. Fail at this mission and suffer the social scars and lacerations from the wounded young cubs.

Connecting the Dots

For many fathers, it may be too late to re-enter the home and the mother's life relationally (and it might not). But it is never too late to be honest with our children and tell them that they are not getting what they deserve. Our "best" has been severely impacted by the way us and their mothers have dealt with one another and from this point on they will only see us deal honorably with women. This little bit of humility, honesty and effort will go a long way. It begins with how we deal with the females around us. Women mostly only adopt free love when grown boys refuse to abandon it. We must seek to understand their struggle. To do this, we will look at the effects the Grown-boy Syndrome has had on females and femininity as we let the record play for the ladies... all my single ladies.

Getting the Big Picture

1. How has the loss of marriage impacted society?

2. In what ways has the decline of marriage in America impacted you?

3. What does marriage have to do with fatherhood and can the two be separated without negative results? Explain why or why not?

4. How could being or continuing to be sexually active outside of marriage affect a person's future marriage hopes?

5. Could being or continuing to be sexually active outside of marriage affect a man's desire to be a good father in the future? If so how?

9 Super Women, Single Ladies & Diva's

What happens when the free love movement wins and women begin to play by the same sexual rules as the grown-boy? I found out in a high school classroom while teaching a lesson on character and stereotyping. One young man raised his hand and confessed, "I think I stereotype females." When asked how, he explained, "I think all girls with tight jeans are smuts." I knew that the term "smut" was Philly slang for "slut." But one young lady vehemently objected, "Hold on, what'chu mean? Just cuz I wear tight jeans don't mean I'm no smut!" Before World War III ignited in the classroom I intervened and asked for clarification just in case they were using the same word in different ways.

At that point another young lady jumped in with, "A smut is a girl that has sex with one guy today, another guy tomorrow, another guy the next day and ten other guys the day after that." I thought that was a pretty good definition. But before I could respond, the first young lady re-entered the conversation with, "No, that's not a smut!" Now just in case I was out of step with the changing culture, I looked around the room to get a visual of the facial expressions of the other youth; their puzzled looks told me that I would be justified in asking, "Oh no? Well then what is a 'smut' to you?" Her response showed that somewhere along the line someone had come in and redefined the sexual terminology for her. She confidently replied, "A smut is a girl who has sex with one guy today, his brother tomorrow, his cousin the next day, and ten of his friends the day after that!"

I was instantly thrust into a state of fright, first for this young girl, and then for our culture. I cringed at the thought of living in a world where there was a difference between those two scenarios, where one would be acceptable and the other deplorable. Once again I looked around the classroom to see if I was alone in my disbelief. Thankfully I was not. And so I asked, still half in shock "Are you saying that the only thing that would make the girl in the second scenario a smut is if the guys she is sleeping with know or have a relationship with each other?" Her response brought tears to my eyes, "Yeah, other than that, she's just a girl who likes sex."

By this point I was dizzy from disbelief; my face grizzly with grief. I don't know if or how I kept myself together except that when she made that justification, I saw half of the class begin to change their minds, looking at one another as if to say, "oh yeah, that's right, I forgot... there *is* a difference." Instantly my mind and mouth went to work in an attempt to rescue and restore these young minds back to a healthier understanding of sex. I began to demonstrate how the terms had been redefined so that what was once dirty has now become decent. I pleaded with the class for them to see themselves as more valuable than current messages in the media and maybe even their upbringing had taught them. I told them that traditionally, a woman was looked at as morally loose anytime she was willing to give herself to a man for less than she was worth.

At that point I asked the class, "What are you worth?" But they were not aware of their true value. "A lot" one of them said. "How much?" I asked. "More than all the money in the world," another eventually shouted. "How much more?" I asked. The class fell silent, wondering, hoping there was a good answer to the question. Every bright young eye glued to their temporary teacher, as if to say, "Please tell me what I'm worth...that I'm worth...." I relieved the built up tension. "You're so valuable. You are worth the rest of someone's life. The only thing someone can give you that's worth *you* is all of them, the rest of them. If they give you anything less, they don't know what you're worth. And if you see someone giving themselves up for less than that, you are looking at someone who doesn't know what he or she is worth."

The young women smiled. The young men blinked hard and long as they computed the data. One of them blurted out, "that's like saying 'you might as well get married first.'" That, of course, was my point. Before I could capitalize on the epiphany, the bell rang and they were funneled back into the world that seeks at every turn, to redefine their experience. As I left the school, I turned on the radio to hear the songs they hear. The tears and grief returned.

Subpar men and Super Women

In the summer of 2009, rappers Lil Wayne, Drake and the Young Money team released the "smash hit" *We Like Her* (and we like her too). The song was not just a "smash" because of its instant success, but also because the term "smash" is urban slang for sex. On the chorus the artists quite crudely and repeatedly admit, "I wish I could f*** every girl in the world." This was the new millennium version of Naughty by Nature's 1991 summer classic *O.P.P.*, except nearly twenty Hip Hop years had gone by, there was no longer any need for euphemisms or abbreviations. Living in a culture full of these kinds of ideas proves to be too much for the average female.

In fact, to properly deal with this, young women need to become super, and sooner rather than later. There was a time when the urban community looked to the traditional grandmother as the super one; the moral center of the family. In his insightful book *Code of the Streets*, Elijah Anderson points out that "the grandmother increasingly emerges as a hero...waiting in the wings and [is] activated by the social and economic crises" destroying the urban family.[1] But the age at which women are becoming grandmothers is decreasing, even as the situations that demand heroism from them are increasing. Women in their early thirties are becoming grand-moms but many are not the super ones we have come to expect, respect and love. It seems women are being kryptonited by the commercial culture in which they were raised. The loss of this kind of hero in the urban community will have a severe impact on the future of the family.

In her song *Super Woman*, Alicia Keys attempts to honor the super role of single mothers. In the video Keys brilliantly conveyed her message by highlighting four women and putting each of their individual accomplishments on the same plane. Most recognizable was Jada Pinkett Smith, the African-American actress/entrepreneur and (married) mother. Another was Nassanga Galabuzi, a Ugandan student, accomplishing her education against difficult odds. Another, Joan Higginbotham, an African-American astronaut. But also, and no less than the others (which was the brilliant point), was Wynter Williams, a mature single mother wrestling through the welfare system while hoping for a college acceptance letter.

All four of these women had to be just as "super" in order to defy the odds against them. Single moms have tremendous odds staring them down every morning and every night, especially if her youth believe they can afford to be "teenagers." Obviously, you only need to be super when you're in the kind of trouble that being normal won't get you out of. Dealing with the grown-boy and single parenting certainly qualify for this.

But being a single mom does not automatically make one a super women. Like every super hero or super heroine there is a story behind how they get their powers. Until the fateful day of the accident or incident which changed them, they are quite normal, almost too normal. In fact, for many single moms it is their all too normal lives, dealing with sub-par men that get them into the trouble which later demands or develops their super-woman strength. If there was a way that she could have been super already; if she could have looked at Mr. Sub-par with an X-ray eye or expert vision, she could have seen the grown-boy in him and avoided the series of unfortunate events that now call for heroism. But because the media often advertises the man-child as the model for manhood, and possibly because her own father was not there to show her true manhood, she falls for the grown-boy's game and begins the tough, transformation process.

Step 1 of the Process

The process begins in what has become a very normal way. We see it all the time. Many people in our society know what it's like to wake up in the morning, lying next to someone they have no real commitment to and no real responsibility towards. They may feel awkward about the lack of commitment or responsibility toward the person, but this awkwardness comes with the territory of free love or what we today call "casual sex." But even when there is a sense of "commitment," but not marriage, many boyfriend-girlfriend couples, and even couples who live together, still sense the awkwardness. For males, this awkwardness manifests as a loss of the drive he once had for pursuing her after sex has been introduced to the relationship before wedding vows are made.

Many young men see sex as the prize at the finish-line after running a relationship race; a race that could potentially go as far as marriage. But if, while running that race, they are interrupted with the gold medals, confetti, and flashing cameras of sexual celebration before ever reaching the finish-line, they hardly run the same; some cease to run at all. And how does this affect the mindset and training of other young men? Free love has produced a society of lazy runners and lousy relationships where no one trains for the distance.

In truth, sex is not the celebration at the finish-line of marriage. Marriage is not the end but the beginning of the race. Professional races begin with a "bang" when the starting pistol goes off. The wedding, the vows, the honeymoon and sex might be compared to the gun going off once the runners are all lined up, on the mark and set. Sex before marriage results in a false start where one or both of the people end up confused about the status of the relationship. There is no community, no accountability; no witnesses to any vows and often very confusing and unequal efforts to keep running or return to the starting line.

This happens as men develop "cold feet" and their will to run "ices up." This causes a woman to respond one of two ways, with *assertive attitude* to periodically thaw him out or with *added attention* to act as anti-freeze. This does not yet make her super; only super sensitive and super insecure, wondering if he will stay in the race after the false start. The first response, assertive attitude, occurs when women become super abrasive, attempting to make the man-child keep his word and carry out his unspoken vows. Unspoken, and yet still communicated since, through the act of sex, his body language practically vowed "oneness" with her, as hers did with him.

In these relationships, the woman practically tries to keep the man-child's commitment for him because he lacks the will to do it himself. She constantly texts or calls and, possibly because he cannot be trusted, he must periodically check in with her as with a parole officer. Think back to our discussion of Benjamin Button, by the end his lover could only cradle him in her arms having turned from lover to mother. This is the dynamic of many relationships in our society where women spend a great deal of time trying to raise their boyfriends.

The second way females respond to the icing up of a man's affection is by paying added attention to his desires and fantasies. The goal is to keep him in the race for her heart or hand in marriage. This is an unsafe scenario for females because it puts them at the mercy of the man-child. Hip Hop has seen its share of females giving this added attention and grown-boys taking advantage of it. Some of the earliest examples include the careers of Lil Kim and Foxy Brown in the mid to late 90s. Their collective contribution to Hip Hop is a stark contrast to Hip Hop's better half during the 80s when MC Lyte, Queen Latifah and Monie Love, commanded respect with songs like *Ladies First*.

With the exception of Lauryn Hill, the female rapper of the 90s was a different breed; ultra feminine and perhaps too feminine for her own good. Her femininity was more for *his* good as was seen in 1999 when rap group The Lox announced, I need a *Ride or Die B***** featuring Eve. This was a changing of the guards for young urban women because for the first time a female MC was actually collaborating on a song where women were being labeled "the B word." Many missed this change because something more important was happening in the song. Namely, men were telling young women what they were looking for in a partner; what she would need to be and do in order to keep him interested. And it worked. Young women paid extra attention and scrambled to become or prove that they were everything the song said.

What the female MC does on record is a reflection of the added attention the average woman offers in her daily dealings with the man-child. More than a decade later the female MC continues to abuse and thereby lose her femininity in order to attract and appease the grown-boy. The beautiful and talented Nicki Minaj stands as the new millennium, prime example of this loss. Once, when asked how she had been inspired by Hip Hop lady legend Foxy Brown, Nicki responded, "the same way [Foxy] inspired every other female...she always held her own with the dudes...when you listen to Foxy Brown with [dudes] you never feel like, 'Oh, here comes the female part.'"[1]

But not only do she and Foxy blend in with the "dudes" when it comes to skill level, they also make it hard to detect the "female part" when listening for lyrics that respect women. Particularly when reading the lyrics of Nicki Minaj, it is often hard to believe that a female could write such words about herself or other females. Because of the strong link between fathers and authors, women are mostly only accepted in Hip Hop when they sound like men or sound like men want women to sound. The fact that femininity has become everything that grown-boys desire is proof that the Sexual Revolution and free love have worked against women and in the favor of men.

Raquel Welch, the woman who helped to kick off the Sexual Revolution in the 70s, sobered up after fifty years of feminist freedom and in 2010 admitted, "Seriously folks, if an ageing sex symbol like me starts waving the red flag of caution over how low moral standards have plummeted, you know it's gotta be pretty bad."[2] After having numerous lovers and having been married four times, Welch blamed society's misuse of the birth control pill for the destruction of marriage and morality. This epiphany came at age sixty-nine after hearing a thirteen year old friend of the family carelessly talk about performing oral sex on various boys at school on a regular basis. Welch's super woman senses were finally kicking in. She espoused, "Marriage is the cornerstone of civilization, an essential institution that stabilizes society, provides a sanctuary for children and saves us from anarchy."

Kryptonite in the Culture

Lex Luther always kept a stash of kryptonite nearby just in case Superman showed up. Likewise, the grown-boy keeps a stash of cryptic clichés just in case women start feeling heroic. The aim is to keep women giving that added attention. There are three such crippling crystals used by modern Hip Hoppers. They have been craftily carved out by redefining three ideas - $ex, sexy and sexuality.

$ex - It was once socially shameful for a woman to put a price on her body and accept money or gifts in exchange for sex. Thankfully, in many segments of society, it still is. But Strip-hop is doing much to take away the disgrace attached this practice. In the fall of 2008, Atlanta rapper T.I. clobbered the airwaves with his hit serenade *You Can Have Whatever You Like*. The song is infectious and those who were not alert probably missed the masterful job T.I. did in pulling a fast one on his lady listeners.

The chorus celebrates what is clearly prostitution, "I want your body, need your body ...you can have whatever you like!" In the second verse he raps about sexual favors he expects to receive and then adds a line that has floated around the Hip Hop industry, "Everybody knows it aint trickin' if you got it," i.e. if the man can afford it, it's not prostitution. For those who may be a little more morally challenged and are tempted to accept this justification, all one needs to do is go back to the beginning of the song where T.I. admits that the coming chorus is a direct quote from "old Sugar Daddies" known for "trickin'" (prostituting) young girls.

What the man-child hopes is that songs like these will successfully redefine what "trickin'" is and erase the stigma that is typically associated with this practice. The hope is also that females will have less reluctance about being propositioned with money for sex. To his credit, New York rapper Fabolous overturned this decision in 2009 when he took his lady listeners on a lyrical shopping spree with the single, *Throw it in the Bag*. On the remix he objected, "They say it aint trickin' if you got it, they lyin'/ I say it aint trickin' if you got *her*, she mine."

Sexy – has also been redefined and has taken the place of "attractive." Especially for females, they must not only have something about themselves that attracts others, they must have something that arouses a desire for intimacy in others. But even more, they must be willing to wear, say or do something that sparks these intimate desires – that is "sexy." Once she gives in to this social demand, she becomes easy prey for the grown-boy and the pressure is always on. When asked, "When does your girlfriend have to be sexy?" one Philadelphia high school student replied, "When she's awake!"

The term "sexy" is synonymous with the Greek word 'eros' from which we get our word 'erotic.' Eros is a lusting type of love that is based on the object, the *loved-one*, having something or doing something that causes the *lover* to love. This is why people can even call cars "sexy" because there is something about the car that causes someone desire to be intimately involved with it – own it, drive it, be seen in it, etc. This is the opposite of the Greek work 'agape.' Agape is a love that does not depend on the *loved-one* having or doing anything but instead is solely dependent on the *lover* as the source of the love. For that reason, agape is said to be unconditional as far as the loved-one is concerned. This is the kind of love ascribed to God in the Bible's New Testament.

In 2009, R&B artist The Dream had a radio killing spree with the song *She Rockin that Thang* in which he sang, "Girl I'm in love with you.../ I'm hooked on your body.../ aint just tryin to get in your clothes/ OK I'm lying but damn you fine." This is love? For superwomen in training, this erotic love seems flattering, but it is flat out kryptonite.

Sexuality - is another area that has been redefined by the creation of a new category for sexual orientation – bi-curious – a term meaning not homosexual, not bi-sexual, but curious enough to experiment. This designation was invented in order to create a bridge for people who were dissatisfied or confused about their own sexuality so much that they are willing to try something different. This removes the social stigma often attached to the subject of same-sex attraction. It is sort of a postmodern concept since it attempts to keep people from being labeled or absolutely locked into a certain category. This explains the appeal it holds for late Generation X and Generation Y'ers.

When a young woman begins to pay extra attention to the grown-boy's desires and fantasies, he can then kryptonite her sexuality. Females have been led to believe that they will be valued more by males if they begin to like girls too. In 2007 Ray Lavender and T-Pain released the comical, culture shocking song *My Girl's Gotta Girlfriend*. In it, once Ray finds out about his girlfriend's friend, he accuses her of being stingy for not sharing the other woman with him. But he will not leave her as long as he can join in the bedroom activity with the two of them. On the chorus he sings, "Two girls is better than none." Rappers frequently brag about getting girls to "go both ways" as Drake does in *We Like Her* as he attempts to pick up a group of females. He hides the question in a clever play on words asking, "are any of y'all into girls like I am, Les-be-hon-est."

Giving into this backfires on the female however. The "man" gets her, but she ends up sharing half a "man" with another woman. Maybe she figures half a man is better than none. Add to this the rapidly increasing number of women making extended visits to America's correctional facilities where same-sex scenarios are commonly played out, plus the number of women who are being turned off by the daily abuse of the man-child, and it is no wonder that we are seeing such a rise of bi-curious behavior among females even at the middle school level. Nicki Minaj, who stated that she prefers girls over boys because boys are "smelly and disgusting and really mean,"[4] represented this new sexuality when she was recruited by

Usher to be his *Lil' Freak*. Her job in the song was to enlist other girls to join her and Usher in the bedroom.

Step 2 of the transformation

When a young woman realizes that the advice of the grown-boy is kryptonite, she turns next to her girlfriends, older female relatives or role-models in the media. One media personality in particular has offered more help than any other women in recent years – Beyonce Knowles. Her musical career has been no less than flawless from the days of Destiny's Child to her solo career which has eclipsed the group's success. After winning the Billboard 2009 Woman of the Year award Beyonce summed up her approach to music, "I always tried to write anthems...my niche is empowering other women; they look up to you for more than just your music or your songs, it's the way you live."[5]

Sometimes though, one wonders if the antidotes she offers are not potent with the same poison that has women seeking a solution in the first place. At first it feels like help. But as the music and medicine go down, things do not really get better, they in fact get worse. Think of some of the bombs Bey dropped on the world in 2008. *Single Ladies* was a bold effort to help women combat the tendency of the man-child to back out of a relationship after it reaches a certain point. For Beyonce, the proper response is to get closer to other men, and when the man-child begins to miss her, tell him that if he liked *it* then he should've put a ring on *it*.

When first asked to identify the "*it*," high school girls give Beyonce the benefit of the doubt and say that she was simply talking about her love, or the relationship. Many confess that after watching the video, it is hard not to see the *it* as her body. At first, the song sounds like a healthy advocate for marriage; but think about what this really means. If a guy has to like *it* before he puts a ring on *it*, then he has to try *it* first. And if he tries *it* and does not like *it*, then he is free not to put a ring on *it*.

If the man-child is encouraged to focus on *it* instead of on her as a whole person, then it makes sense for him to try several people's *it* in order to be sure that he is getting the best *it* that he possibly can. But this does not help women. It backfires and ends up putting even more pressure on them: first, to let him try *it*; and second, to do whatever possible to make sure he likes *it*. This is certainly guaranteed to fail more than succeed as was evident in a radio interview with Hip Hop sensation Drake in June of 2009. Drake had recently released the "smash" hit *Best I Ever Had* in which he raps/sings "I want this forever; I could spend whatever on *it*." The type of girl he is referring to sexually pleases him "every time" he calls but makes him "beg for *it* til' she gives *it* up." And each time he says to her, "You're the f***ing best I ever had." This is the chorus!

Drake called in to Philadelphia's 100.3 FM for a radio interview during which the host, Pooch Man, asked whether the song was about anyone in particular. Drake responded, "This song is about a mixture of girls that I've had. And also, it's about a girl I haven't met yet." This should be a wakeup call to females that letting "men" try *it* is not going to produce the results they desire. Drake had experienced the "best" he'd ever had in a mixture of females and was still looking for the best he hasn't had yet. In 2010, singer Lyfe Jennings, known for warning women about the grown-boy, tried to help women identify Mr. Right with his song *Statistics*. In it, he advised women to tell potential mates, "I'm celibate, and if you want some of my *goodies* you're gonna have to work for *it*." This is not celibacy but sadly, marriage is nowhere in his list of helpful hints, so this is the best advice he can give.

All of this keeps women at the mercy of the man-child.

Putting a committed marriage based on character before sex could save her from this. Young people have hatched their own plans to try to accomplish the aims of marriage in a different way. Some have bought into the idea of a promise ring where boys are told, "We can't do 'certain things' until you give me a promise ring." This attempt at a makeshift marriage lacks the logistics of the real thing. True marriage has several safeguards. First, through things like pre-marital counseling, couples are forced to honestly assess whether they have the character it takes to keep wedding vows. It is foolish to ask someone to make wedding vows when they do not have the character to keep them. It is also cruel to expect someone to keep wedding vows that they have not made. Both the commitment and the character are key.

Considerate: You care about what others need and how your actions affect them

Honest - You tell the truth, even when it hurts

Altruistic – You are willing to make personal sacrifices for the good of others

Responsible - People can count on you to do what is required of you

Accountable – Making yourself answerable to others

Consistent - People can expect these qualities from you on a regular basis

Trust-worthy - People have good reason to trust you.

Exemplary – You live a life worth imitating

Reliable – People can count on you to do what is expected of you

Integrity – You are whole morally, not lacking essential qualities

Self Control – You govern yourself according to intellect, not impulse

Kindness – You show compassion towards others

Ethical – You know and do what is most right

Yielding – Willing and able to compromise with others

Marriage does not make people all these things

People who are all these things make marriage

Second, marriage (done right) has accountability; the welcomed eyes of others in our community. This also helps us live up to our vows. Accountability helps after the wedding but also beforehand when choosing a partner. Sadly, instead of welcoming the eyes of concerned friends and family it is more common to hear, "I don't care what my friends tell me" as in Ciara's 2007 release where she pledged her allegiance to the street hustler/drug dealer, singing, *Can't Leave Him Alone* because The *Dope-boy's Turnin Me On.*

In an indictment against the grown-boy, Beyonce hit a homerun with her song *If I Were a Boy*. In it, she tells the man-child that if she were a male, she would be a better man than he. However, at times, Beyonce stands up for women, but then in a confusing attempt at street credibility, she sounds as if she has caught the grown-boy syndrome herself and stands for the man-child.

In the 2008 anthem *Diva*, Beyonce flashes the textbook definition of a Diva at the beginning of her video; she then spends the next three minutes redefining it, just as the grown-boy would. Of all the people she could have chosen for the Diva's new identity, surprisingly, the Diva is now "the female version of" a very familiar character – the "Hustler." Hustler, in hood vernacular, is simply the term used to refer to anyone who is serious about getting money by any means necessary. But more specifically, the hustler is someone who often has an illegal agenda to get legal tender. Drug dealing is most commonly referred to as hustling. Next, working barely legal jobs, such as selling CDs or DVDs (often without permits or permission) is considered hustling. Then lastly, working a legitimate job can also count as hustling, but the term loses some of its semantic force when it refers to strictly legal activity. But for Bey, the Diva is now a hustler.

I do not believe that Beyonce means to directly advocate illegal activity. It is likely that she chose the word because it could carry either of the two meanings, illegal or legal hustling, similar to conscious rapper Lupe Fiasco when he gives a shout out to his "homies out there grindin', legally and illegally." After all, Beyonce did marry Jay Z, the "monster of double entendre." But double entendre is an intended pun where someone means to convey both of the possible meanings, not just one. If this is what Bey intended, it would be a bit scary, but it would also explain why she celebrates the diva's hustle by singing lines like, "This is a stick-up I need them bags...that money... You see that mask, where dat money?"

The "Diva" apparently has something in common with the hustler; either they are both making money, or they are both taking money. But the song is crafted so that whichever version you like, it works for you. For many young girls who have resorted to "thuggin' it" in order to attract grown-boys looking for a *Ride or Die Chick*, this song was their anthem too. Put together, the *Diva*, who believes she could be a better man than the man-child if she *Were a Boy*, turns around and gives a thumbs-up to the man-child by making the *Diva* nothing more than "a female version the hustler." Once again, the solution contains the sickening syndrome.

The only way musical artists can get away with such irresponsible lyrics is by ignorance or arrogance; but those are luxuries only the rich can afford. They can lock their car doors and drive past the neighborhoods where their lyrics are lived out. Neither ignorance nor arrogance gets a grown "teenager" off the hook when the consequences for their actions catch up with them. The question is often asked, "Why are rappers and singers in the urban market judged for violent lyrics or held to a higher standard than actors in violent movies? Isn't it the same thing?" But Beyonce has already told us her lyrics are, "more than music." In Hip Hop, people are not claiming to be actors.

Jay Z, in his *Encore*, claimed that when he returns like Jordan with his own 45, it won't be to "play games witchu" but to "aim atch" and blow you to "smithereens." Young Jeezy challenged Nas in the interview mentioned in chapter 3. While Monie Love was trying to get respect for Nas because of his tenure, Jeezy had a different set of criteria which, in his eys, deserved more respect. "Has Nas did anything he talk about? [Does] Nas bust his guns? [Has] Nas been on the block? Do Nas have street credibility? Is any of Nas' homies in the [Federal penitentiary]?" This shows that Hip Hop and Hollywood are not made of the same stuff. Although it may be easy for Bey and Jay to cross the tracks from one side to the other, as they sang in one of their hottest duets *Hollywood*, the vast majority of their listeners remain trapped on one side, with no directors to yell for the cameras to cut. They must keep it 100 percent, all the way real.

But even in Hollywood, an artist's words can come back to haunt her. In 2009, Beyonce teamed up with Kanye West for the braggadocios ballad *Ego*, where the two celebrated their huge sense of self. Months later, she, along with the rest of Hollywood and the world, was left speechless (literally, since she was later compelled to give her acceptance speech time to Taylor Swift) when Kanye stormed on stage, ripped the mic from Taylor Swift during her acceptance speech at the VMA awards and proclaimed that Beyonce should have won the award instead. One can only wonder how much she loved his huge ego when she, in super woman mode, was forced to clean up behind the grown-boy West in his black designer (Benjamin) Button-up top.

Connecting the Dots

Finally, this all fails us. Older grand-moms, like the heroic type mentioned by Elijah Anderson at the beginning of this chapter, were produced as grandchildren multiplied and grandmothers were called on for moral or financial support to stabilize the family in times of need. Today's single moms have a different road to super status: doing the job of two people alone; raising the "men" they love or his children, or both. If mom manages to raise her children well, sacrifices for them, keeps her dignity and self respect, furthers herself in the process and learns how to resist the man-child, her growing children will recognize her strength and rely on her continued assistance and painfully won wisdom for help with the grandchildren. She is super woman.

But just as the grown-boy is getting younger every year, so are today's grandmothers.   Younger grandmothers means that more and more, we will see new matriarchs from the generation that failed to catch the baton from the Civil Rights generation, and along with the baton, the morals and values it takes to be women of character. Instead of being the moral center, grand-mom will be self-centered on the postmodern edge of "do whatever's right for you." Instead of caring for and nurturing others with wisdom, grand-mom will be self serving and pleasure seeking but rarely finding happiness and not very super at all. With grand-mom unable to play her hero role, the future is not bright for the urban family. And things will only get darker unless we can bring the culture back to a state of consciousness and reawaken one of the only heroes left in Hip Hop,   the   conscious   MC.

Getting the Big Picture

1. How has the Sexual Revolution worked out in favor of men?

2. If there was a way to ensure that men would be just as faithful as they expected women to be, do you believe that women would have still fought for free love? Why or why not?

3. Should it matter that 1970s sex symbol Raquel Welch now has negative things to say about the Sexual Revolution she once endorsed? Why or why not?

4. What would you tell a young woman who is considering making sex a part of her relationship:
(a) build a friendship/relationship without sex until marriage
(b) Wait until you find true love
(c) You'll never be able to trust men so just take a chance and make sure you use protection

10 Supermen, Consciousness & Contradiction

Where are the supermen; the heroes of our day? If we ever thought things were bad enough, what symbol would we flash in the sky and who would come to the rescue? If a hero actually came, what problems would he address? On the title track to his 2006 comeback album *Kingdom Come*, Jay Z compared his return to the timely arrival of Super Man, Spider Man and Bat Man when signaled for help. "When you need me" he told fans, "just throw ya Roc[-a-fella] signs in the air." Jay announced that he was "not only NYC's but Hip Hop's savior."

In an interview for his 2010 album *Thank Me Later*, rapper Drake explained that hopeful listeners looking for him to be "the one" to save Hip Hop would be obliged to thank him later as they grew to appreciate his contribution over time.[1] Both Jay and Drake embraced the role of hero but only as far as the musical aspect of the culture was concerned. Are there any heroes left in Hip Hop who see themselves as more than merely the music's messiah. And if so, who are these supermen and what's keeping them from swooping in and saving the day?

First we must answer the question, "who aren't they?" In the first chapter we discussed the role of the traditional NAACP. The organization's youthful president, Ben Jealous said, in true superhero fashion, "Wherever injustice is, we'll be there, on the watch." In an interview with CNN's Don Lemon entitled, *The "New" NAACP* Jealous talked about the new dangers facing his generation and why the NAACP was still needed:

Our generation knows in their hearts, that as much as we have benefited from the dreams of our ancestors and all of their hard work, we're the most murdered generation in this country; we're the most incarcerated generation on the planet. When you think about who's going to fight those battles, it's hard to imagine unless the NAACP is in full effect.[2]

The segment emphasized the word "new" not just because of Jealous' age but also because the biggest struggle of minorities in America is no longer from without, but from within. Today's struggle involves issues of character, values and morality. But unless Ben Jealous makes extreme efforts to change the focus of the organization, African American's will not look for the NAACP to spring into action on these inner issues. We will continue to flash the symbol for the NAACP when we have outer issues, such as racial inequality, like the Jena Six incident. But what hero does the post civil-rights generation look to for help when it comes to inner issues – problems with the man in the mirror and the culture on the corner? It is none other than your friendly neighborhood conscious rapper. This was the case in 2009 when 16 year old Chicago student Darrion Albert was murdered by rivaling teen gangs. In seeking answers, many, including CNN, turned to conscious rapper Common for insight into the inner issues of urban youth.

Knowledge is Power

Three things allow us to view the conscious rapper as the super hero of our day as far as Hip Hop is concerned: The conscious rapper fights real evil, has real power and gets real respect. Let's look closely at each of these.

1. Real Evil. Hip Hop has helped to cultivate the evolution of "hate." It began when rappers developed their own version of the old model's motto, "Don't hate me because I'm beautiful." In 1999, rapper Ice T granted his foes permission to

Hate the Playa. Later that same year Nas and Puffy's told us you can *Hate Me Now.* Since then, it has become normal to label anyone who is not a diehard fan of yours, a "hater." In 2008, rapper Maino released the song, *Hi Hater,* which spawned the T-shirt [Hi Hater – on front; Bye Hater – on back]. Even grandmothers could be seen sporting this flippant T.

One reason people liked this theme is that it felt good to finally have an identifiable, beatable enemy when facing the challenges of everyday life. If my real enemy is simply that person at the club who's looking at the same guy or girl as me, then I can overcome them by being a better dresser, flashing the keys to a better car, or simply labeling them a "hater." And just like that, I've won! Pop another bottle and let's celebrate. In their songs, most popular rappers post up against some perceived threat, a "hater," and then musically murder the imaginary enemy.

The conscious rapper however, can be credited with actually addressing real issues. He is not imagining evils to overthrow, instead he looks to shed light on the destructive forces in our world: be it injustice, ignorance, intolerance, indifference or just the inability to cope, as in Talib Kweli's *Just to Get By.* In 2010 Kweli returned with the single *In This World* where he identified the character traits of "pride" and "laziness" as the real enemy to be destroyed. To be a real hero, one must fight real problems; therefore the conscious rapper hardly spends time talking about haters. For him, there are bigger fish to fry. But fighting these real problems can be difficult. For this, real power is needed.

2. Conscious rappers have real super powers. To be a super hero, you have to be able to do more than the average citizen, and for that, you need strength or ability that regular people don't typically have or tap into. Most, if not all, known conscious rappers will look beyond themselves (or within

themselves) to the realm metaphysical realm for strength. The word metaphysical means, 'beyond the physical.' It is the acceptance of the idea that there is more to life than just the physical world that we experience with our five senses.

Metaphysical is the realm of the "soul" where words like "spiritual," "God," "right," "wrong," "truth," "meaning," "purpose," "destiny," "karma" and "believe" are often heard. The people who don't mind tapping into this realm have several things in common. First, they have come to the realization that something is fundamentally wrong with us as human beings. We often do things we say we didn't want to do, and the things we want to do, we don't always do.* Because of this tendency, people either hurt themselves, or the people they love, or the people they are supposed to love. This demonstrates that something is broken, and needs to be fixed. This is why the "self-help" section is one of the most published, furnished and trafficked sections of any bookstore.

Another thing that is common among those who look to the realm of metaphysics is the belief in the idea of an ideal or "should be" world. They have in their minds and hearts a vision or version of the world that is much different from our present reality. And not just different, but better; and not just better, but so much more "moral" that they believe our present world "should be" more like their ideal world. They believe it is not just possible, but that it has been prescribed by some metaphysical reality – a god or an over arching design telling us how the world "should be."

But who or what is this god or design beyond our physical world? That depends on who you ask; nonetheless, the metaphysical person says we are robbing ourselves of real peace and true joy by not making our world an exact copy of

---

* The Bible, Romans 7:19, 20

their ideal world. He or she looks to bring that ideal world to bear upon this world, as in the Lord's Prayer, "Thy kingdom come, Thy will be done, on earth, as it is in heaven."*

3. Super hero respect. When watching movies about superheroes, one thing you hardly ever see is the hero's help refused. The hero is always welcomed and at times, he is sought. When Hip Hop has troubles of a soulish nature, the conscious rapper is sought to enlighten us, or comfort us, or correct us. The conscious rapper has enjoyed a certain level of honor and respect, both on the celebrity stage and in ciphers on the street. The entire mood in rap circles of young MCs changes after a conscious rapper injects his brand of lyricism. The next rapper to go after him is hesitant to use the word "nigga" or too much profanity. Whoever follows him usually begins with the disclaimer, "my raps ain't all like yours." This is an acknowledgment that maybe their raps "should be" like his.

Respect comes with the territory. This comes from the recognition that conscious rappers are ultra-talented; many of them are some of the most skillful lyricists alive - telling stories, conveying abstract concepts, working with and playing with words to construct elaborate metaphors for life. The respect comes also from the fact that these artists have not "sold out." Clearly they have the skill to make money like the rest of mainstream Hip Hop, but they also have the character to stand on principles that keep them from doing things their consciences would later regret. Because their consciences are so strong, we have unofficially elected them to be our collective conscience – conscious rappers serve as our conscience's rappers.

In an interview, rapper 50 Cent attempted to brand himself a conscious rapper for a different reason. "They say I'm

---

* The Bible, Matthew 6: 5-15

a gangsta rapper, but I consider myself conscious – cuz I know what I'm doing."[3] However, the concept of a conscious rapper is not just that the artist knows what he is doing, but that he cares about what he is doing. And his conscience would be bothered if he were to do certain things. We have looked at the three things that raise the conscious rapper to the height of a hero. Now we must look at three things that bring him back down to earth and keep him from properly playing his hero role: Superfluous Supermen; Self Sabotage; and Self Censorship.

Superfluous Supermen

Perhaps you have heard the story of Buddy. Buddy was an enthusiastic little boy; maybe a little too enthusiastic. But whatever his flaws, one thing's for sure, he knew how to pick his super heroes. He had chosen the greatest hero for his role model. He followed his hero around whenever he could, often showing up uninvited, only to find his hero less than happy to see him. Buddy even had his own super hero outfit, but to be honest, there was really nothing super about him. Often his hero would tell him, "Go home Buddy." To which the boy replied, "I can help you." "I don't need help Buddy." Still he offered, "I can be your sidekick." His hero shot him down again, "I work alone."

If you follow animated movies, you know this is a scene from one of the most acclaimed, *The Incredibles*. As the plot thickens, the film resembles the trouble facing our own conscious rap heroes. Later in life, Buddy and his hero Mr. Incredible meet again, but the later encounter is a bit more interesting. Some time goes by and due to several unfortunate events, Mr. Incredible, along with other real super heroes, was forced to go "underground" (like many conscious rappers). Buddy however, had not been completely idol, wasting his teenage years. After designing two new inventions, he brings them to the attention of the now outdated Mr. Incredible.

The first invention is a gigantic, destructive robot that only Buddy understands; and the second, a set of gadgets that will allow Buddy to easily defeat his engineered enemy. His plan is brilliantly diabolical. First, he will let the destructive device loose on city streets, allowing it to wreak havoc on unsuspecting citizens. Then, Buddy will show up as a new kind of super hero. He will use his gadgets to defeat the problem he caused and people will see him as a "hero." This sounds very much like the average rapper dealing with his "haters." He is not solving anyone's real problems. He wants so much to be super that he has created an imaginary enemy in order to defeat it with his own lyrical weaponry before our very eyes. And we applaud him for his victory.

Buddy then reveals that there is a commercial side to his evil scheme. After he has had his fun and enjoyed the super hero rewards and respect long enough, he will sell his invention, both the problem and the solution, so that anyone and everyone can become super. He tells Mr. Incredible why he wants to do this: still scarred from the fact that his father figure/hero Mr. Incredible dismissed him as a child, the only way to get the attention he wanted was to become "a problem." Buddy now hates the idea of there being any super heroes at all.

He figures his problems will be solved if everyone becomes super in a superficial way. Because, "When everyone is super," he schemes, "no one will be." Buddy wants to flood the city with a surplus of "sort-of" supermen because if everyone is defeating their own imaginary problems, thanks to their new "special" store bought abilities, then real super heroes won't seem so special anymore. The best part for us is that Buddy has a new name. There is now an "S" on his chest. Not for "super." No - Buddy is now a grown-boy named Syndrome. Was Hollywood trying to tell us something?

The conscious rapper is hardly seen as a hero these days

because in many ways, everyone has become super. Conscious rappers already had to compete with record labels who heavily invested in more commercial versions of rap. But with all of the gadgets available today, anyone can become a super-star. In 2007 *Time Magazine's* Person of the Year was "You." Instead of a photo of the year's honoree, there was a reflective square on the cover for the reader to see him/herself. They said that because of YouTube and MySpace and other online tools, people no longer need companies and corporations the way they used to. You could pretty much do it yourself. Advertising companies are competing for business with the average Joe on YouTube who can make a commercial for McDonald's just the same and for less money too.

The good thing about this was that we began to hear talented artists whom we may have never heard of if we had to wait for a record label to sign them. The bad thing was that we also began to hear from others whom we would not and should not have heard from due to their lack of talent. Jay Z even put out a dis record called *Death of Autotune* because the recording gadget helps people with no singing ability to sound as if they can sing, allowing many to become super singers and rappers at the expense of real artistry. With all of these gadgets, anyone can become a temporary star. They don't last long, in fact hardly anybody does; there is always another upload to check out even as you are in the middle downloading one. There is a surplus of singers, rappers, producers...you name it. Everyone has become super. But if everyone is super, soon, no one will be.

Self Sabotage

In his book *The Hip Hop Generation*, Bakari Kitwana observed that "When it comes to gender issues, Hip Hop generationers are willing to overlook the dark side of their heroes."[4] But it seems that Hip Hoppers will overlook any fault whatsoever, unless we are talking about the faults of the conscious rapper. He cannot escape because the conscious rapper claims to stand for something. Because he stands, he is more visible when he falls short of some standard he has set or suggested. The terms contradiction and hypocritical are thrown around a lot on this point. In the interview with 50 Cent mentioned above, he demonstrates how contradiction brings many would-be or could-be conscious rappers back down to earth. Speaking of Kanye West he states that people called him conscious "but only because of *Jesus Walks*, [but] he'll follow up with a record like *Gold Digger*, that doesn't coincide with that conscious title."

On the ultimate dis track, *The Take Over*, Jay Z tore into Nas for falling off the rap scene and challenged him to switch up his flow; he questioned Nas' efforts at trying to "kick knowledge," an old school reference to conscious rapping. It has long been public opinion that the Achilles' Heel in Nas' career has been his stabs at consciousness, seen through his nicknaming himself "god son" and posturing himself as a type of prophetic voice for the streets; followed up by contradictory acts, such as his songs *Oochie Wally* and *You Owe Me*, in which he told women that they will owe him sex once he spends money on them.

Rap battles are often good for calling attention to the contradiction of the could-be conscious rapper. In the legendary dis record *2nd Round Knockout*, Can-i-bus "went in" on rap icon L.L. Cool J for "frontin' like a drug free role model." Can-i-bus reported, "I know B****es that seen you smoke weed recently." In the genesis of the East coast – West coast beef, Common convicted gangsta rapper Ice Cube for his contradictory stance; not because Cube was a gangsta rapper; that was fine. But Cube had recently begun to stand with Lewis Farrakhan and the Nation of Islam, and still went on to do campaign ads for a brand of malt liquor that exclusively targeted the inner-city. On the dis record, *I See the B**** in You*, Common labeled him a "hypocrite" for "slinging bean pies and St. Ides in the same sentence" and questioned the concept of a "Muslim drinking brew."

It seems the more metaphysical the rapper, the more contradiction we can expect. Blast Master Kris aka KRS One has been flagged for several logical fallacies, not the least of which was his attempt to cite the Bible for contradictions in his song *The Truth*, only to turn around years later and record a Christian rap album. In the process, Kris sought to do collaborations with Christian rapper T-Bone as well as with my group, The Cross Movement. We were honored by the chance to speak with Kris about our similarities and our differences however The Cross Movement did not participate in the album. The finished product was a metaphysical montage of mixed messages. But Kris seems ready for this charge. In his song *The Conscious Rapper* he prepares other would-be heroes, "To be a conscious rapper aint a mystery," and encourages them to "laugh when [people] call you contradictory."

One of the most honest expressions of the contradiction that causes these heroes to stumble comes from one of the most gifted conscious rappers to date, Lupe Fiasco. In his song *Hurt Me Soul*, he confesses to being a Jay Z fan, but being turned off by Jay Z's famous line "I never prayed to God I pray to Gotti." Lupe asked God, "guard me from the ungodly." But after watching Jay Z's independent film *Streets is Watchin* over thirty times, Lupe admits, "I was back to giving props again."

While searching for the right record label and deal to fit him, there were talks of signing him to Jay Z's Rocafella Records. Rumors have circulated that Lupe did not feel that the conscious music he made would work well with what Jay's label was already known for. Nevertheless, Jay Z executive produced Lupe's first album from afar.

In an interview with 247HH.com, Lupe gives us a prime

example of the conscious rapper's capacity for contradiction. When asked a question about racism he responds:

> Rascism exists, it built this country. It's necessary, it's a necessary evil... But I hate it. I wish that we could obliterate it. But that's not gonna happen...we're all a product of racism...the only way that's gonna stop is the next generation has to grow up unaware of separation...of any type of classism or any type of economic difference that's specific to a particular group of people...they can't have that history...so we have to now [say] you know what? We're gonna deprive our next generation of history. Are we ready to do that, are we ready to say "No slavery, no Ku Klux Klan, none of that existed. This is a world now where everybody lives in harmony and peace." I don't think we're gonna do that cuz we got too much pride. Pride comes from our history...so we wanna teach kids so they can't forget but when you do that you inject racism into them.[5]

Then, when asked about leadership, Lupe criticizes Al Sharpton for wanting to abolish the word "nigga" and adds:

> I love the word 'nigga'... cuz it represents our history, it represents this country, it represents what it's about, so why would you abolish that. What type of leadership is that...to obliterate our past like that...that's wack as hell.

It becomes hard to listen to our conscious heroes due to the lack of consistency in their message.

Self Censorship

The last reason conscious rap super heroes are hard to find is because many of them censor themselves. Not that they don't exercise their freedom of speech. They do that very well. What many of them are more reluctant to do is exercise their freedom to preach or responsibility to teach. The best conscious rappers do an excellent job at shining light on what is not right in our world. But few have taken that extra step of telling us what we should do differently. Somehow they feel the responsibility to creatively warn us that a train is coming, but not an obligation to follow with, "Get off the tracks!" Many fear being labeled "preachy." Again, Lupe Fiasco shows us the timidity and trepidation with which conscious rappers struggle, walking on eggshells. In his song *Trials and Tribulations*, Lupe tells us he aims to "shed light on troubled youth" and "explain all their grooves and roots" but "not enough to incriminate, just enough to demonstrate."

This hesitation to do anything more than "demonstrate" only reveals that many rappers do not understand that the MC has in fact become this generation's baton. In chapter 8 we saw the connection between authors and fathers/leaders. In the 18th century, Irish political activist Daniel O'Connell coined the phrase, "Let me write the songs of a nation, I don't care who writes its laws." He understood the importance and influence of writing, especially when writing something in a form that is more likely to be read or heard, such as a verse of song vs. a book of laws. Songs are more powerful than laws but what if they are not as moral? And while we're on the subject, whose morality should we judge them by? These questions of morality and authority keep the conscious rapper's voice to a whisper.

Supermen, Philosophy and Psychology

We began this chapter with the question, "Where are the supermen, the heroes of our day?" This question was asked by German philosopher Friedrich Nietzsche in 1883, in his work, *Thus Spoke Zarathustra*. Nietzsche believed that certain events (which we will discuss in the next chapter) had made it necessary that supermen should arise and rescue humanity from its fatal outlook on life. To him, the superman's job was to instruct mankind in a way to live that would create and enhance life; sort of like what the "father" or "author's" job was. Before losing his mind to a psychotic breakdown, Nietzsche spent the last years of his life writing, trying to help his fellow Germans grasp the idea and power of the superman and why one was needed so badly. Nietzsche wanted to see people become super without looking to the metaphysical or religious realm in order to get their "powers." He wanted a "should be" world without a religious reason for it. For this reason, Nietzsche would not have liked our conscious rappers.

Philosophy is not alone in its attempt to deal with supermen; psychology has spoken of them as well. All of the psychologists who've helped shape the way we think about human thinking have developed some type of explanation for why we often feel that things "should be" different or better than they actually are. Consider Albert Ellis' Rational Emotive Behavior Theory. He believed that any attempt to live as if things "should," "must" or "ought" to be a certain way is irrational thinking. We should accept things as they are and not desire them to be otherwise. If we cannot do this, Ellis says, we are trying to live as "super-humans" by controlling what cannot be controlled.[6]

Nietzsche wanted men to become super so that things could be different; Ellis wanted men to stop pretending they were super and just accept things as they were. After years of dealing with conflicting assignments like these, our supermen don't know what is expected of them. Hollywood has even caught up to our confused superhero. In the 2006 film, *Superman Returns*, the hero tells his leading lady Lois Lane, "You wrote that the world doesn't need a savior, but every day I hear people crying for one." Interestingly, Superman returned to find that he and Lois had a son who was being raised by another man. Superman in the new millennium was an absent father, relationally removed from his son's mother.

Connecting the Dots

Our writers and rappers are playing roles they don't fully understand. They feel the great power, but not the great responsibility. The conscious rapper walks on egg shells, silencing himself while the gangsta and thug rappers raise our youth. In *The Incredibles*, the grown boy, Syndrome resurfaced at the end to steal Mr. Incredible's infant son. This is indeed happening in real life. The grown-boy syndrome is stealing the nation's sons. Women are struggling to be super while commercial industries are profiting off of the plight of the inner-city.

Our "supermen" and "superwomen" resemble Will Smith and Charlize Theron in the 2008 film, *Hancock*. They were male and female super beings, created in pairs. But as super as they were, sadly, the closer they got to one another, the more mortal they became. For them, intimacy meant death; made for one another, and yet no good for each other. The only hope was for them to separate. Maybe that makes for a good movie, but in real life this is the furthest thing from "good." We are being kryptonited by bad definitions of the word "good." "Good man." "Good father." "Good relationship." "*Good Good*," if you've heard singer Ashanti's pitch. We need an upgrade. Our conscious rappers would be more consistent, and even the thug and gangsta might grow if we could agree on a post-postmodern meaning of morality. In the next chapter, I would like to introduce us to a greater good, a new morality.

Getting the Big Picture

1. From what has been stated here or from your own observation, why does the conscious rapper not get more light in modern Hip Hop culture?

2. If conscious rappers were heard from more often, do you think their message would:
    (a) be mostly about social injustice; e.g. the economy, government corruption and police brutality
    (b) address the behavior of young fathers toward their children
    (c) address the behavior of men in our society toward women?

3. Which do you think is most important and why?

4. How would you define the words "right" and "good"?

Part Three

IMMORAL MORTALS
&
The MORAL IMMORTAL

11 *MORE*-ality - What's Really Good?

What's up? What it do? What's poppin'? What's good? It seems that out of all of the urban "hello's" over the past 40 years, the progression has finally led up to the most important question that can be asked by anyone alive today, be they Philosopher or Philly Hip Hopper. "What's Really Good?" This quintessential question has been asked countless times on the street level and received the most unfitting answer in response, "Aw man, it ain't nuthin'...I'm just chillin'." Before we deal with why this response is so unfitting (and it is not for the lack of proper English), we must first deal with the key word in the question – "good." What is goodness and how do we know?

Thanks to postmodernism, it is no longer acceptable to use the words "right" and "wrong." Instead, it is better to say that something is "more desirable or less desirable – to me, or to us," so that we do not offend those who might disagree. But if there really is no such thing as "right" or "good" then there is no real "wrong" or "bad." In that case, how do societies decide what will legal and illegal? When we sentence criminals, how do we know we are not just punishing them for going against our personal preferences and desires? What about the criminal's unpopular personal preferences and desires – don't they now count if there is no "good or bad," "right or wrong"

Is a child really "wrong" for talking out of turn or taking what is not hers or causing another student to be in some sort of pain? Detention rooms and disciplinarians are nonsensical ideas; rigid rules and definite deadlines are just subtle suggestions and general guidelines if there is no authority on the subject of right and wrong. Clearly, society is suffering from such a suffocation of the virtues, even as media voices are turning up the volume on the vices. If we ever wanted to, would it even be possible to regain our sense of good?

Where did good go?

In 1882, German philosopher Friedrich Nietzsche imagined a fictional character he called, the "mad man," who gladly grieved while making the announcement that "God is dead." He claimed, "We have killed Him" with our humanistic (man-centered) reasoning and philosophies. In reality however, Nietzsche was first in line when it came to getting started with the solemn celebration of the Death of God. Upon his declaration of the divine death, two philosophical groups formed and have been growing ever since. On the one hand, there are those who attempt to attend the philosophical funeral of God and slip a few of His old "favorite things" into the closing casket to be buried along with Him. On the other hand, there are some who realize that those "favorite things" of his could still be very useful for those of us who are still alive.

As this second group eyes the lowering lid and locking latch of God's colossal coffin they are plotting how they might return to God's grave and dig him up, hoping to retrieve those precious pearls of wisdom that have been buried with him in the earth, or in the heavens, or in our inner-selves, or wherever it is that we have laid God to rest. But just what are these gems of God? They can be summed up in one word - Morality.

Is it possible to have morality without religion? Nietzsche believed it was. He challenged his audience to produce this, saying that they would have to be supermen, almost godlike, to accomplish this task. In 1929, the British philosopher Bertrand Russell took Nietzsche up on this challenge. Russell announced a "new morality," one that directly addressed the issue of sex and marriage. "The old morality we get from religion" he claimed, "will no longer do." His solution to the old, "out-dated" morality of monogamous marriage was either: allow the state to step in and take over the financial obligations of the father, thereby freeing men from their familial roles and responsibilities; or open marriage up so that wives and husbands are equally, sexually free to love other people, but remain a family for the sake of children.[1]

Almost a century has gone by and it seems we are arriving right where Russell predicted. His "new morality" was masterfully weaved into George Clooney's 2009 film *Up In the Air*. The idea behind the film was that only children maintain boyfriend-girlfriend relationships; while true "grown-ups" get married, have families, stay together as companions, and have extra-marital affairs to relieve the pressure of all that "real life." But we must ask if this "new morality" is actually "moral" in the first place.

If you had to define morality, or even something as simple as the word "right", where would you begin? You would likely start by using several words interchangeably – right, good, best, and moral. Eventually, you would sink into using a different set of words, such as – most people, most of the time, common opinion, and general belief. The Encarta Dictionary makes a similar shift. Notice their first definition for the word "right" - *Accurate, or consistent with the facts or general belief.* Now, being "consistent with the facts" works, but agreeing with "general belief" is not the same as being right.

If general belief says that black people are only 3/5 of a person (as America once decided), does that make agreeing with such a belief "right?" Hopefully you are saying, "Of course not!" But can you go a step further and explain what you have based your "Of course not" on? To say that something is wrong automatically means that something else is right. And once you say that, someone is going to stand and ask, "Says who?" or

"What are you basing that on?" The answer to these challenges is usually some form of dogmatism (because I say so) or pluralism (we're both right, even if we disagree – just do what's right for you).

Consider the Encarta Dictionary's third definition for the word "right" - *correct with regard to use, function, or operation.* This is closer to where I believe we are headed. It syncs with the Greek philosopher Plato's definition of good. He claimed that something is only good to the degree that it accomplishes the end for which it was designed. So then, according to Plato, in order to decide whether something is right or good, we must know the purpose of the thing, and take it from there. Are the following things good?

Guns Sex Marriage Money Politics Drugs Human Beings

Try to come up with a purpose for each of these. Plato's view says, you must not only think of the purpose, but how well each thing is accomplishing its purpose. Let's focus on human beings. What is our purpose?

Can we agree on a purpose that even the postmodern person can accept for his or herself? We might accomplish this and unlock *endless potential for progress in our lives, relationships, society and world* by taking a closer look at the word "moral." Why? Because that is precisely what moral means. Where do I get this definition from? Follow me for a moment and we are sure to arrive at it. Frederick Nietzsche claimed that "God is dead." Let's pretend that we are among those who wish to exhume the excellent ex-Deity in order to retrieve some of the buried treasure from his rich religious record.

I believe we can find the basis for our understanding of morality early on in the pages of the Bible. In the creation story of Genesis chapters 1 and 2, every phase is followed by the phrase, "And God saw that it was good." The first time we see the phrase, "It is *not* good," is after God created everything else in the universe, when he looked at the man he made and pronounced "It is not good" followed by the words, "that man should be alone." Adam also looked around and saw that every other living creature had a partner with which to create more life, and yet he himself had no one to help him with his task. This was the first thing that was said to be "not good" in God's world. God addressed the situation by putting Adam to sleep, splitting his side, removing his rib, and "cloning" him a soul mate.

Once they were man and woman, God gave them an important job that says a lot to us about the purpose of mankind and morality. "Be fruitful and multiply, subdue the earth and fill it." Theologians refer to this as the "cultural mandate." Their job was to take the life God gave, and take it up a notch. As the first marriage, they were to multiply by having children. As groundskeeper of the Garden of Eden, Adam's job, with Eve's help, was to keep the fruit and vegetative life increasing, without letting anything die. And as for their responsibility toward the rest of the earth, their job was to take over and show the planet what its Creator was like by representing him on every part of it; taking what was and making it into more.

Adam alone, unable to accomplish this was "not good." When God looked at their joint potential, it was all good. They could maximize on the endless potential for progress - personally, relationally, socially, environmentally, holistically. You could call it the perfect combination of capitalism and communism - capitalize on every opportunity for the advancement of life, but for the sake of every part of creation and eventually, every created person. The goal was always "more," a planet full of abundant life. Today, we still see mankind's built-in desire for *MORE*-ality. In our society it manifests itself in men seeking to acquire more, always building something; and women seeking to adorn more, always beautifying something.

But notice what "good" in Genesis did not mean. It did not mean to just keep things the way they were. It also did not mean that after things start off good, it's okay if eventually *Things Fall Apart* between men and women, as Hip Hop/soul band The Roots warned us. That would have been unacceptable. Also, good or moral, in Genesis does not simply mean more lives, it means more life! Not just quantity (the number) of lives, but quality (the nature) of life. This does not mean adding more things to one's life. By now it should be quite clear that adding new possessions is certainly not the same as adding life. In fact, gaining more things could actually lead to less quality of life, especially if people have to give up parts of themselves or deprive other people in order to get the things they desire. "Be fruitful and multiply" is a command to only add without letting anything die, like Adam in his garden. This is morality.

There really is no such thing as a morally neutral activity. Even resting is moral because it allows us to evaluate and enjoy what we have worked on and without rest we cannot be as effective in future adventures of adding. We are always either adding, being added to, taking away or being taken away from. Adding is moral, taking away is immoral. In the Bible, "sin" is no more and no less than disagreeing with God about what adds to life; trusting our impulses and intellect instead of his input and intentions.

Added to that

Is there any support for this definition outside of the Bible? Perhaps. Is it merely a coincidence that the words *more* and *moral* sound so similar? What if they actually share a romantic, semantic relationship? Two Greek words and a newly coined Latin word might support this speculation. The Ancient

Greeks used the word "moros" to mean great, or greater, from which we get our words, "more" and eventually "most." Another Greek word, "ethikos" was used to mean – *The proper behavior of a person in society*. When the Romans came and conquered Greece, they thoroughly embraced Greek logic, language and literature. Rome sought to translate much of Greek writing into Latin, but the word ethikos was difficult to capture. What Latin word could be used to convey this important Greek concept? The answer was provided by one of the greatest Roman orators, Cicero.

Cicero was regarded as the chief public speaker and prose writer of his time. He introduced his fellow Romans to the various schools of Greek philosophy and even created a Greek to Latin philosophical vocabulary. Cicero, the skilled linguist and philosopher, even with his vast knowledge of both languages, still thought it necessary to coin a brand new term just to bring the meaning of "ethikos" over into Latin. The new word was "moralis." The word also appeared in Latin as moris and mos. We still use the plural form of the noun, mores.[2] This is where we get our words "morality" and "ethics" from. What was Cicero telling his Roman world about the nature of ethics in a society? Was he attempting to build on the easier to understand Greek word moros (more) as the root for his translation? Was he in effect saying, "True ethics is seen in ideas and actions that produce a sense of more-ness; *MORE*-ality; a growing degree of life throughout society?"

In the 1969 best-selling self-help book *I'm OK, You're OK*, Thomas Harris laid out two forms of social interaction, or two ways that we impact one another in society through what he called "transactional analysis." Harris says that when we come into contact with another human being, we either have a "crossed" experience, where one or both of the people feel slighted or snubbed or subtracted from in some way. This leads to a ceasing of the conversation. Or, he says, interactions that are not crossed are called "complimentary," meaning they add to one or both of the individuals. Elaborating on this, Harris says these "adding" interactions can go on indefinitely (without end).[3] This shows that even in a postmodern world there is still a built-in link between adding more and morality. We are not completely in agreement with everything in Harris' book, but at least on this point, he has added something valuable to our discussion. We might even say we have had a "complimentary" interaction with him.

Measuring Morality

"Moral" carries with it the idea of lengthening and strengthening life. But long life by itself is not moral. Just look at the Bible's 5th Commandment to "honor your mother and father so that your life may be long *and* go well with you." Obeying parent's moral instruction does not just lead to long life (quantity) but "good" life (quality). This leaves us with several interesting questions. If something both adds to life and takes away from life; is it moral or immoral? What if it is moral, adding to life, for me, while taking away from someone else?

People answer these questions based on ethics. Ethics refers to how someone weighs or measures morality. We will look at three distinct approaches to ethics and how they each show up in the media; they are ethical egoism, utilitarianism, and deontological ethics.

1. Ethical Egoism - Think of measuring morality as a ruler with twelve square inches (Figure 11.1). Each square inch represents a unit of "goodness" or the amount of life being added by making a certain choice. Our first approach to ethics is called **ego**ism because it only focuses on the self. Whenever an ethical choice must be made, such as, whether or not to send text messages while driving, egoism asks "How many of the squares on the ruler represent more life for me?" If more of the squares represent the advancement of the self, then it is considered a good or moral choice. If some of the squares happen to produce less life for someone else who I am not connected to, that is not my concern.

Some have argued that society only works because we are all a bunch of ethical egoists who cooperate with one another only enough to get our own needs met. They say society would stop working suddenly if tomorrow each person woke up, looked at the moral ruler of personal choice and saw nothing good on it for themselves.

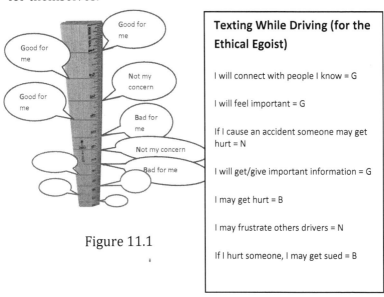

Figure 11.1

That is a frightening thought which may have some truth to it, especially for many who follow Maslow's bottom up approach to life. Egoism happens to go hand in hand with the postmodern world-view.

For the most part, the ethical egoism of people around us is tolerated until it affects us personally. But egoism can be affecting us without us even knowing. For instance, we allow people to harm themselves and say things like, "to each his own," and "hey, as long as she's not hurting anybody (other than herself), then it's ok." But this fails to take into account how she is hurting others by hurting herself. Not just because people care for her and do not want to see her harmed; but also because whenever a person does something to him or herself which makes them less available (emotionally, physically, mentally or spiritually) they are no longer present and able to add to what is. Life immediately becomes less moral for all of us when people are absent from the adding process while busy harming themselves behind closed doors.

2. Utilitarian Ethics is another approach used to measure morality. Instead of focusing on the self, this approach focuses on society as a whole, or at least on the bigger picture of all the known variables. Instead of being a ruler with twelve square inches, utilitarianism sees each moral choice more like a square foot, full of 144 square inches. (Figure 11.2) The first row may still be the 12 square inches of the egoist's ruler, but the remaining squares represent others who might be directly or indirectly impacted by the decision being made. If more squares represent positive results for more people, then the choice is moral. If however, more squares seem to represent negative, life lessening results for more people, then the decision is immoral.

Based on this view, when a decision has to be made people say things like, "do it for the greater good" or "choose the lesser of two evils." One of the good things about utilitarianism is that it moves us past the selfishness of egoism. This allows society to function with some degree of confidence that people will not simply drop out of trusted public positions precisely at the moment it ceases to benefit them personally.

However, I can think of three critiques of this approach that should caution us against relying on it wholeheartedly:

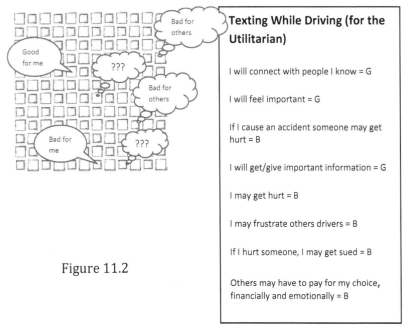

Figure 11.2

1.) It ignores the personal interest of the minority. If the majority of people will benefit from a certain decision, and they have the power to make that choice on behalf of the minority, the few people in the minority will lose to the desires of the majority. American slavery has been cited as a case where this ethic produced results that should have been viewed as immoral. Even though more people benefited from it than not (whites vs. African slaves) that did not make slavery a moral institution. Thus, utilitarian ethics could be seen as "group ethical egoism."

2.) If all moral choices are weighed this way, it could lead to the questionable practice of judging the morality (goodness) of individual people based on this same ethic. In other words, if a person's good outweighs their bad, then they must be a good person, right? This sounds logical at first; however it is not a simple task to verify the sincerity or true nature of a person's good deeds. To do this we would have to know the motives of their heart. In addition, it is impossible to trace and tally up the extent of damage that results from even just one of a person's bad deeds. Let alone the ripple effect of every immoral act and decision they ever made. So, it is impossible for us to know if a person's good really outweighs their bad.

3.) This approach assumes that we are able to see all of the angles and account for all of the possible consequences and outcomes of a certain act or decision, which again, is humanly impossible. If we live by utilitarian ethics, we must be willing to live with certain consequences, even the ones we could not or would not see from our vantage point.

3. Deontological Ethics – the last of the three that we will consider comes in two flavors: Universal principle (such as natural law) and "Divine command." Universal principle simply says there are certain things that are universally right or good and others that are universally wrong or bad, no matter where and when they happen. Most people who hold this view will put rape and murder in the "universally wrong" category. Someone who holds this view might say, "Nature just has it so that things work a certain way and if you act against nature, then it is wrong." The person who objects to this view will ask, "Where do you get that from and who says it's wrong? I can understand you not liking something, and if we all don't like it then let's make it illegal. But you can't call it wrong because nature doesn't have a right or wrong. Like tsunamis and earthquakes, nature just is, and we just are."

These are good objections, which lead us to the other flavor of deontological ethics – Divine command. This approach is found in major religions that say we have been told what is right and wrong, not by a universal principle, but by an unequaled Person, namely God. This system has benefits and a few drawbacks worth discussing. One benefit is that it saves us from having to figure out all the pluses and possible negative outcomes of a decision before we call it moral or immoral. Nor do we have to worry about the angles we can't see because someone who can see all of the angles has already spoken on the matter. This takes the pressure off.

The drawbacks are: first, I have to trust that some divine entity has spoken on the issues at hand. And if I care enough to know, I must now search to find out which supposed divine discourse I will follow. Another drawback (that could actually be a plus) is that divine-command ethics is not just a square foot with 144 square inches of moral concerns; instead it is a three dimensional squared cube with length, width and height (figure 11.3). The first line of longitudinal squares still represents my egoist concerns. The latitudinal squares deal with my social relations with the rest of the world. But the vertical squares represent my personal relationship with the divine-command-giver, which is a blessed relationship if all the squares are moral but a broken relationship wherever the squares are immoral. This puts the pressure back on.

Figure 11.3

Texting While Driving (for the Deontological Ethicist)

Do unto others as you would have them do unto you – *Matthew. 7:12*

Obey laws of your land that don't contradict natural or divine laws – *Daniel: 6; Acts 4:19; Romans 13:3 ,4*

Be about the business of adding to life without taking anything away unnecessarily – *Genesis: 1:28; 2:15*

Avoids the moral guessing game

Morality in the Media

These three ethical systems show up in the media all the time. If we stick with our theme of superheroes, two Hollywood films will suffice. In *Spiderman (Part 1),* Willem Dafoe played a riveting Green Goblin. At the movie's climax he taunted Toby Maguire's Spiderman character saying, "This is why only fools are heroes - because you never know when some lunatic will come along with a sadistic choice." He said this having rigged a streetcar trolley full of children to drop into a river while at the same time, Mary Jane, Spiderman's girlfriend, dangled over the same river.

Which of the ethical systems discussed above would have made it easier for Spiderman to choose to save Mary Jane and which system would have made it easier for him to choose the streetcar full of children? Of course, Spiderman the ethical egoist would have saved Mary Jane, the love of his life. And Spiderman the utilitarian would have had no problem choosing to save the streetcar full of children, since that would have benefited more people producing the "greater good" or the "lesser evil." It can be argued that the writers were pushing us toward the deontological view of natural law which says that "all life is sacred," since rather than making a choice, Spiderman saved both Mary Jane and the kids in the streetcar.

Next, in what has been called one of the best superhero sequels to date, *The Dark Knight,* Christian Bale ignited the role of Batman. The movie included a climactic scene similar to Spiderman's moral choice. The villain this time - the Joker, played by the late Heath Ledger, arranged to have two large boats filled with two, seemingly very different, kinds of people. One boat carried ordinary city folk, just going about their daily lives. The other boat, convicted criminals in orange prison jumpsuits, chained hands and all. Both boats were rigged with explosives but each boat had a detonator designed to explode the other boat. Their moral dilemma – blow up the other boat or get blown up by them. And if neither boat had the courage to do the deed by midnight, the Joker would explode them both.

Think about the scene for a moment, once again all three ethical systems are in play. Which ethical system was the Joker counting on in this insane social experiment? Which ethical system do you think movie goers were leaning towards as they watched the scene play out? And which system won? The Joker assumed that everyone, when forced to make that kind of decision, would take the egoist position which says, "if it's either me or you that's gotta go, you'd better say your prayers!" Movie watchers probably wrestled with the utilitarian "greater good" concept which might make it easier to root for the law abiding citizens instead of convicted criminals; but this also ignores the rights of those affected by the decision.

But fear not, Hollywood once again pushes us toward a mysterious morality. The writers seem to support the universal principle; some kind of natural law that secures the sanctity of human life. Neither boat was morally able to destroy the other. In fact, on the criminal's boat, the actor Tommy Lister's intimidating character approached the fearful, morally confused prison guard holding the detonator and told him, "Give it to me and I'll do what you *should* have done 10 minutes ago." He takes the device and throws it out of the window then returns to what looks like a prayer huddle.

The fact that Lister's character used the word "should" reveals the belief in a real "right way" and a real "wrong way" to behave in this situation, not simply a personal preference. To the writers, there was something wrong about taking life in this scenario. It would not have been self defense for one boat to destroy the other since the Joker, and not the people on the other boat, was responsible for their present danger. Also, there was no way of knowing whether the people on the other boat intended to use their explosive device. Each boat had to trust and hope that the other boat would do the "right" thing, the "moral" thing. When no one died, Batman told a surprised Joker, "This city just showed you that it's full of people ready to believe in *good*."

Movies often show us deontological - natural law ethics when it comes to things like murder and rape. Natural law may also be used to address lying and stealing. But natural law seems to be silent on the subject of relationships and sex. The deontological – divine-command ethical systems speak to this issue but it seems Americans are moving away from traditional religious beliefs and practices that "fit neatly into conventional categories." This way divine-commands will have a hard time reaching them. In December of 2009, the Pew Foundation released a national survey which found that:

> Large numbers of Americans engage in multiple religious practices, mixing elements of diverse traditions. Many say they attend worship services of more than one faith or denomination....[And] though the U.S. is an overwhelmingly Christian country, [a surprising amount] profess belief in a variety of Eastern or New Age beliefs. For instance, 24% of the public overall and 22% of Christians say they believe in reincarnation. And similar numbers (25% of the public overall, 23% of Christians) believe in astrology. ... and 15% have consulted a fortuneteller or a psychic.[4]

But even if we could completely move away from or silence the divine-command-giver, nature is not completely silent about our relational and sexual mores, it speaks to us through our consequences.

Side-stepping the Superlative

The great philosopher Walter Kaufmann believed that mankind evolved from apes, yet he marveled that man is such a "God intoxicated ape," consumed with religion. As history and even current culture shows, something from within pushes and at times, pulls us toward a deontological, divine-command view of ethics. Does taking the deontological view make egoism or utilitarianism wrong or unnecessary? Ethicist Scott Rae has suggested that the God of the Bible actually appeals to His people on all three of these ethical levels.[5]

Whatever the case, it is clear that ethical egoism and utilitarianism are short sited when detached from deontological ethics. Even for people who hold to Judeo-Christian views, deontological ethics became deathly difficult duty after "the Fall of man" in Genesis 3. Some combination of these ethical systems seems necessary. Deontological ethics, when properly combined with egoism, can teach me that even though life is about God's story and not mine, still, my role in God's story is most blissful and blessed if I live according to his moral code. If I disagree with him about what is moral, then I become immoral, not living more, but living less. This means that the egoist cannot even be a true egoist without the divine-command because he will be oblivious to what actually works out best for him and will miss out on a relationship with the Author of the ethic.

True morality, *MORE*-ality, sees a series and then seeks the superlative – good, better, best! But that was before the "Fall." After Genesis 3, morality morphed. What's best is no longer the moral standard. We have come to settle for what's good enough. In chapter 8, we talked about settling for being a "good enough" father. Not the "best," but "good" or "better than" our own fathers were. This is utilitarianism - the lesser of two evils or the greater good instead of true *MORE*-ality which is "no evil" and "the greatest good."

In chapter 4 we briefly discussed capitalism and communism. Capitalism is really just an attempt to ensure that society is full of productive (moral) people. It operates on the ethical egoist assumption that if people are going to get more out of something, they will pour more of themselves into that thing (e.g. career). But instead of being productive, the goal often becomes to get more, at any cost. In 2010, oil giant BP was making 93 million dollars per day when their negligence led to the deep water oil spill in the Gulf of Mexico, which killed eleven people and changed the way of life for residents along the Gulf Coast. Competing oil companies had been cited for as little as one and as many as eight safety violations over a five year period. During that same time, BP was cited for 760 egregious and willful violations with indifference or intentional disregard for employee safety and health.[6] For them, more was not based on *MORE*-ality.

Communism approaches things from the utilitarian view and tries to get people to be productive and do what is best (moral) not just for self, but for as many people as can possibly be accounted for. But those at the top of the system are often egoists who manipulate things to their own advantage and to the detriment of others. Pastor John Piper uses a different barometer when he states, "Man is most satisfied *when* God is most glorified." Instead of pleasing self or the majority of the people, looking to please God first would accomplish both of those aims.

Connecting the Dots

What's really good stems from deontological dependence on the divine-command-giver. With all of your talent, attractiveness, money, opportunities, relationships, goals, wants, appetites, etc. will you trust Some-one to tell you how to live, or will you trust yourself, believing that you see enough of the angles to make the moral choice? Without the deontological approach, morality degenerates into opinion and preference, which eventually turns into anarchy and chaos.

One of the greatest Christian minds ever, Augustine, completely allegorized Genesis chapters 1 and 2 at the end of his classic work, *Confessions*. My mind is not quite as great, so I will not allegorize quite as much, but maybe a little. Genesis 3:15 is not just about the eating of fruit from a forbidden tree. That is not why Christians believe we are in this mess. This story was not recorded in scripture to teach us about a greedy, petty God who refused to share his fresh fruit. Instead, the garden, the trees and the fruit are perfect pictures of life and growth – *MORE*-ality. Add to that the divine-command by God not to eat from one of the trees, which was rooted in the knowledge of good and evil (the ability to determine what is life lengthening and life lessening); along with the warning that disobedience would bring death; and another tree rooted in eternal life; all of this combines to produce the mother of all object lessons.

The lesson was really an invitation. It was God saying, "What I command is ethical – the way you are to live in society. My ethic is true *MORE*-ality. How much more? So much that it leads to everlasting life. But disagreement with Me about what is moral, about what adds more life - is immoral; and only leads to death. Therefore, get to know me as the One with the knowledge of good and evil. Let me be God."

Today, politicians, philosophers, teachers and parents – can all be found amongst that group of desperate individuals looking to dig up some kind of divine morality that rises above egoism. Recently, some have even forged a new path in ethics calling themselves "principled humanists." These are people who still hold that God is dead and that mankind is the measure of all things, but they have become willing to admit that there must be some overarching moral principles on which we can all agree and by which we can all live. But principles apart from a purpose, a design, a Designer, a Person, are hard to hang on because someone is always going to ask, "Says who?" And how will we respond?

Perhaps, we are beginning to regret that we have killed God. We have buried him in our past, and it's just our luck; the morality we so desperately need is tucked underneath his heavy, Holy Ghost in his star-studded, cloud-covered casket in the sky; buried too high for us to dig him down. What type of morality will we have now? What's really good?

Getting the Big Picture

1. What is the author's definition of "good"? Do you agree with this definition? If not, what is your definition of "good"?

2. Would it be good if the state were to step in and do the financial job of fathers, thereby freeing fathers from their role? Why or why not?

3. Bertrand Russell (and others) believed that instead of trying to control the great emotion of love by forcing married people to be faithful, we should be learning to control the bad emotion of jealousy, and allow married spouses to love other people outside the marriage. This is how he would save marriage – would this be good? Why or why not?

4. Which is more loving: for married couples to allow one another to love other people; or for married couples to go on forsaking other potential loves for one another? Explain your response.

5. Which ethical system discussed in this chapter do you most often operate according to?

6. This chapter looked at the potential moral dilemma of texting while driving according to three highlighted ethical systems. Discuss the morality of sex outside of marriage according to each of those three systems.

12 Immoral Mortals

In the suspense thriller *The Sixth Sense*, Bruce Willis played a child psychiatrist out to help youth with their mental meltdowns. After failing to help a particular teen, the youth returned one night and shot Willis at point blank range. Several months after the shooting, Bruce Willis' character was back at it; helping another child with similar issues. But this child confessed something eerily strange to Willis, "I SEE DEAD PEOPLE." Willis asked, "Are there any in this room now?" "Yes," the child's head signaled. The boy explained, "They only see what they want to see; they don't know that they're dead." Throughout the movie Willis offers his help, unsuccessfully trying to console the child's mother and being there for the terrified child as much as possible.

There is distance between Willis and his own wife. They don't speak. They can't connect. Finally, as the movie's twist is revealed, Willis comes home one night to find his wife on the couch watching home-video footage of their wedding day; when they were happy. She has fallen asleep. Suddenly, something rolls out of her hand onto the floor. It's a wedding ring; but not hers – his. His un-beating heart stops as he remembers the words of his patient, "I see dead people...they don't know that they're dead." All this time Willis has been fruitless in his attempts to console the boy's mother, and unable to connect with his wife, terrorizing the child he was trying to tranquilize, all for one simple reason - He had been dead ever since the gunshot in the opening scene.

Bad News

This scenario perfectly matches our situation and there

is both good news and bad news for us all. Of course, we will unpack the bad news first. The bad news is that, like Bruce Willis, we are not alive as we suppose, in fact, we are dead people. Sure, we exist. But what does it mean to be alive? Speaking of his cigarette addiction, author Russell Hoban once said, "I don't feel as if I'm living unless I'm killing myself."[1] If we need to come close to killing ourselves just to feel alive, then maybe, we don't really know what it is to be alive. In fact, rather than saying we are living, wouldn't it be more accurate to say that we are dying? Each year, each month, each week, every day, with the passing of every hour, every second...with each breath, we are one step closer - breathing to death.

Is this simply a pessimistic "glass half empty" outlook? That depends; the glass is half full if it is being filled. But if it is being emptied, then it actually is half empty. What about us? Are the hour glasses of our lives filling up or fleeting away with the sands of time? Unless some miracle has occurred, you do not have more life left now then when you woke up this morning. We are what we call "mortal." Mortal means destined to become less and less until we are no more. "Mortality" refers to how close a creature is to death. But what most do not realize is that there is a direct link between immorality and mortality.

We can define immorality according to each of the ethical views in the last chapter. According to the deontological divine-command view, immorality is disagreeing with the divine-command-giver about what is moral. In the utilitarian view, immorality is anything that takes away from the overall scheme of life more than it adds to it. Immorality according to the egoist's view is anything that does not work out best for one's self, but remember what we have said; without the deontological twist is the egoist is robbing herself of a relationship with the divine-command-giver and by doing this, creates lesser life for herself. Causing lesser life than what could or should be is the meaning of immorality.

Can we really say that it is immoral to allow oneself to settle for a lesser version of life? What if someone doesn't want more life? Should they feel bad about not being as moral as they could be? We can answer these questions from the deontological view. The Bible's Genesis chapter 11, records the famous story of the Tower of Bable where God is said to have scattered men into many nations. The text says that men wanted to huddle up and build a monument to themselves rather than do what God commanded Adam and Eve, which was to spread out, subdue the earth, increase and multiply, capitalizing on the creation by represent him in every part of it.

When men chose to keep things small, central and locked up within themselves, God's solution was to confuse their languages, causing them to scatter and get back on the mission of *MORE*-ality. This attempt and failure was supposed to lead men back to God for his moral instruction. This is perhaps where our moral and cultural confusion is leading us today. It is too bad however that just as we are realizing our need for God we are told that we have killed him.

But if God could speak from beyond his glorious grave (for even in death, wherever God is, there must be glory), he would likely say that simply settling for 'what is' still takes away from life because it is taking away from the possibilities of 'what could be.' In basic biology we are taught that anything that does not grow is not alive. This is why we naturally look for growth in our lives and the lives of others.

You may have experienced that awkward moment when running into an old friend from school and the question is asked, "So, what are you doing these days?" Whoever is still doing the same things as they were "back in the day" feels a bit embarrassed. Why? Because there has been none of the expected growth. Something within us longs for *MORE*-ality. If this is so, why do we have such a hard time with it? It is simple; because we are immoral. And because we are immoral, we are mortal. This is what God told Adam and Eve in Genesis 2, 'When you stop believing Me about morality – what it takes to live, you will surely become mortal – you will die.'

Proof of Death

In the movie *Proof of Life*, Russell Crow and Meg Ryan teamed up to tell the story of a woman whose husband had been kidnapped in Mexico. Meg Ryan hired Crow to get her husband back safely. There was a $600,000 ransom demand for his release and safe return. Once in command of the ransom negotiations, the first thing Crow did was demand proof of life; a picture or something to show that the kidnapped husband was still alive and worth ransoming. The kidnappers demanded a small sum of money for the proof but Russell Crow denied this request, saying they should provide proof of life for free; he called it a show of "good faith." Hold that concept for a moment and think about our own kidnapped culture, our country, or for that matter, all the continents combined.

If some alien agent were to ask for proof of life in order to determine whether or not planet earth was worth rescuing, do you suppose that we would be able to produce any? The outlook is grim. It seems that we more easily produce proofs of the opposite. In the film *The Day the Earth Stood Still* an alien race observed planet earth from space, and rather than coming to rescue or ransom us, they determined that our humanity was so horribly morbid as to justify the destruction of the human race. Other films have similar themes. In *Equilibrium* and *I Robot,* in order to save ourselves from disaster at our own hands, mankind must either give up being fully human or surrender being in control of our own freedom – otherwise we are doomed. These films suggest that the problem is in our nature – we are immoral and therefore more mortal than we can ever imagine.

If Genesis chapter 3 could speak to us, it would suggest that man's spiritual power cord has been ripped from the socket and the source of our morality was cut off from that point onward. But if this is true, how is it that we are still able to look so lively and pull off so many mini moral missions all over the map? Remember what happened in January of 2010? Haiti experienced the devastation of a 7.0 earthquake. The world financially responded out of a sense of "moral obligation," forgiving Haiti's debt, raising and donating funds and superstar singers and rappers re-recorded the *We Are the World* single for Haiti's sake. Doesn't all this prove that we are still morally alive? Not necessarily.

Have you ever turned off a ceiling fan, and even though you know it's been turned off, you question that fact because it takes its time slowing down enough for you to be sure? You can still see the effects of the fan around the room; papers are still blowing in the breeze, the air is still cool from the oscillating blades. But, it never fails, eventually the blades become less busy; they become boring. You can count them if you wish. Finally, sadly, all motion dies down and comes to a halt.

So it is with us. Our world is still spinning, but haven't we been dying down for longer than history records? Sure, we are still able to breeze over to this or that place; we come up with newer, cooler inventions, but doesn't our addiction to immorality and mortality follow us into each new area of human achievement? There are too many examples to name but let's look at a few.

Take for instance – cars. It may sound strange, but Bertrand Russell suggested that part of the breakdown of the family and sexual morality can be blamed on the production and popularizing of the automobile.[2] Before cars, young men had to date and court young women in the presence of other (older) people. This kept the relationship at a safe pace. But after automobiles hit the street, things sped up. You may recall old movies where "teenagers" borrowed dad's car and went to places like "Make-out Point." The term "rocking & rolling" was originally a euphemism for sex and it just so happens that the first recorded Rock & Roll song, *Rocket 88*, was about a car.[3] Today, many rappers brag about what single ladies do for them in the public privacy of their cars. In his song *Parking Lot Pimpin'*, Jay Z bragged that he turns "automobiles to hotels on wheels."

In the documentary *Indie Sex II*, film industry insiders discussed the movie rating system and how impossible it is for regulators to keep up with our social mores. Critic Matt Singer sung the praise of "the human spirit," because "no matter what technological advance we invent we will almost immediately discover a way to sexualize that advance." These advances in technology end up becoming accomplices to our immorality. The world-wide-web is certainly no stranger to our immoral initiatives. Lil Kim and T-Pain demonstrate this on their duet *Download*. It is insulting, or else the epitome of ignorance, that with all of the sexually motivated assaults and child predators lurking online, not to mention people whose whole worlds have been ruined because of inappropriate images ending up in the wrong hands, somehow Kim and Pain were still able to sing about being "up all night having cyber sex" with a person they've never met, sending erotic pictures to cell phones and setting up sexual rendezvous with new found internet friends.

Think this song is only for responsible adults? Think

again. The video shows eleven year old child-star Khamani Griffin supposedly stumbling upon an unguarded computer where startling images had been left on the screen by "grown-up." But amazingly, this is not shown as a potential negative consequence of cybersex; instead the youngster ends up dancing to the carelessness of his care-givers.

It doesn't stop there. Our cell phones have become hell phones. We cannot function without them. This great technology is now the suspected culprit for several life-lessening events. In a piece entitled *Intextication*, NBC's *Today Show* reported on a Virginia Tech. Transportation Institute study which found that drivers were "worse when texting than when drinking" and that texters where twenty-three times more likely to have an accident.[4] This has not stopped immoral motorists from messaging. Train conductors have missed their cue because they wouldn't miss their call and caused catastrophes coast to coast. Beyond that, we are no longer present with the people around us in social settings; instead of adding to their lives we belittle them by choosing to talk to or text people who are nowhere near us.

Still not convinced? The link between our immorality and mortality is stunning. Businesses, banks, borrowing and buying are drying up, largely because of greed, selfishness and the lack of self control and accountability at every level of the financial sector. As a result, our economy is dying. During the 2008 financial crisis that crippled America, thirty-one Security and Exchange Commission (SEC) employees, responsible for policing Wall Street were too busy to do their job. What were they doing? One senior official was busy viewing pornography eight hours a day, storing boxes of downloaded material in his office. Another was denied access to adult websites 16,000 times. An SEC accountant attempted to access adult websites 1800 times in two weeks and had over 600 pornographic images on her computer.[5] This was only one percent of the government agency's 3500 employees, but seventeen of these individuals were senior officers and as we have said, anytime even one person is not morally present, life immediately becomes less moral for the rest of us.

We see married and unmarried romantic relationships failing and families fracturing at an alarming rate. This is a major area where our immorality shows up. The staggering number of STD cases among teens and young adults in America, even in the face of bold condom ads, reveals the even more staggering truth that, even though we say we are "living it up," sexually we are dying. This is yet another area where we don't know how to live. This last point deserves special attention considering the fact that we live in such a sexually active society.

Beware of ads that don't add

An ad for Trojan Condom's "Evolve" campaign showed a bar full of women getting "hit on" by pigs; literally, curly-tailed, pink pigs trying to pick them up. The background song sets the scene, singing the pig's pick up lines. In the song, a woman tells one pig that she'll only give him a chance, "when pigs fly." So what does the filthy animal do? It goes to the bathroom and buys a condom. Instantly the pig is transformed into a desirable man. He comes back to see if his new, condom carrying swagger will do the trick...it does. She's blown away at the "new and improved him." The background song wraps things up neatly with the words, "Look at me baby, I just got wings." But wait. What just happened? The pig flew. It "evolved" and grew wings. How? Because instead of being a filthy pig and sleeping with a woman it just met, now it's going to do it with a condom! And Presto! No more pig.

Here is proof of death in several ways. First is the fact that we are defeating the purpose of sex. Do we realize what we are saying when we talk about using "protection?" We are seeking protection from the most supreme act of intimacy. Intimacy means, nothing between us that stops us from sharing ourselves (emotionally, mentally, spiritually, physically). Protection means, barrier, guard, shield, defense. Put together, this means that we are seeking to put a barrier and a shield in the middle of an act of sharing ourselves; what a backwards concept. The reason why sexual education that promotes condom use has not stemmed the tide of teen pregnancies and STDs is because we crave intimacy, not protection from it. "Safe sex" strikes the mind as "Ludicrously contradictory," Scott Rae quotes:

> Sex can be many things: dark, mysterious, passionate, wild, gentle, even reassuring, but it is not safe. If it is, it is not very likely to be sexy. How to abandon oneself to another, how to give your body into someone else's care and control, and remain safe? Sex is dangerous. It's supposed to be.[6]

The psychological thrill of sex is in believing that you've found someone you can trust with the most dangerous form of intimacy there is. But the joy of sex goes beyond simply believing this to knowing this and knowing that they are willing to trust you too. The only real safety in intimacy does not come from condoms, but from the morality of the commitment of true marriage. The more safe we try to be outside of this, the less intimate the encounter. This is why C.S. Lewis defines sexual morality as, "Either marriage, with complete faithfulness to your partner or else total abstinence."[7]

Second, this ad represents an invasion of privacy. The tag line at the end of the commercial says, "Use a condom, every time." This means that every time someone wants to have sex they must get Trojan or some other condom company involved. In an age where parents cannot tell children to wait for sex, Trojan can? But why do these condom companies want to be a part of every sexual experience? Is it because they care so much about our safety? Possibly, even though condoms are not 100% effective against anything they aim to protect us from.

It could have something to do with the fact that the condom industry is a $400 million dollar industry.[8] Even the ones distributed for free in clinics and schools are being paid for, in many cases with tax payer money as organizations like Planned Parenthood continue to receive the lion's share of government funding for sex education. We need a new sexual morality or else we will continue to add to our immorality and mortality.

Lastly are the names associated with all of this. The original Trojan horse was not about protection, but deception. Inside the gift of a wooden horse, an army of enemies snuck into a fortified city and attacked it. Is this what sex is? Receiving an unwelcomed guest who is only acceptable because of the cover-up? We welcome the Trojan "gift" knowing that behind the disguise lies an untrustworthy individual. The name of this ad campaign was "Evolve," a word which means to change, grow, advance and go forward. This sounds a bit like our definition of moral. But our need for condoms to keep us safe from intimacy is proof, not that we have evolved, but that we have devolved and gone backwards.*

In 2010, a South African doctor invented a female condom with hard plastic teeth in order to help local women deal with the insane culture of rape and violence in which they lived. The device inflicts maximum pain on would-be sexual attackers. In our society, the teeth of the contradictory idea that we can get close enough to have sex with someone, but not trust them enough to actually be intimate, should be biting into our collective consciousness telling us that we are doing something

---

* A committed married couple seeking contraception is not the same as two sex partners trusting condoms for safety because they cannot trust one another.

"wrong."

Mortality: A Self-Righteous Reflex

Immorality means that our moral meters or our will to act morally, or both are broken. Because of this, we often hope that Nietzsche was right, that we have killed God and he will never be able to judge us for our immorality. But even now, we are being judged by the natural consequences of our immoral acts. And even when nature takes too long, we judge one another in matters both great and small. We judge self-righteously of course, believing that we should be quickly forgiven for our immorality. But when it comes to others, we are quick to call out the executioner.

Since immorality sooner or later leads to mortality, we find ourselves pulling the plug and pronouncing death sentences on things that contain immorality. This "death reflex" is a natural instinct in response to the immorality of others. For instance, lying is immoral because it kills trust and confidence, which are needed in order to morally strengthen relationships. Laziness is immoral because it kills creativity and service to others. Therefore lying and laziness are discouraged in hopes of destroying such immoral traits.

Kids know about this "death reflex." They experience it when they play organized games and feel that something unfairness has been allowed. They threaten to quit the activity which usually results in the other party "fessing up" saying something like, "alright, alright come on, it's your go. I'll respect your call." Adults do it too in social settings such as on the job when they feel someone is showing favoritism or using a double standard. We may not use the terms "right and wrong" or "good and bad," but we cannot deny that these things suck the life out of us and zap our desire to remain in those situations. Immorality ruins trust, joy and peace and eventually results in the death of any activity it is found in, and depending on how important the activity was, it can even alter or end relationships.

During the height of the hippie movement there was a bold demonstration of the fact that immorality leads to mortality. After the Summer of Love the Haight-Ashbury neighborhood that hosted the free-love festivities was left with massive homelessness, drug problems and crime. On October 6th 1967, those who were sober enough to recognize the gross after-effects staged a funeral for what they called the "Death of the Hippie."

Years later, Mary Kasper explained the funeral saying, "We wanted to signal that this was the end of it, don't come out. Stay where you are! Bring the revolution to where you live. Don't come here because it's over and done with."[9] It is interesting that after seeing all of the social destruction that came in the name of hippie "freedom," she could still encourage people to bring "the revolution" to where they lived. By doing this, she practically pronounced a death sentence on any city that may have taken her up on that immoral offer. This makes Nas' 2006 *Hip Hop is Dead* claim even more interesting. Was his funeral procession subconsciously recognizing that immorality had led to the culture's mortality?

Less is the New More

Through technology, we are constantly adding to our world. But what if we are actually adding things that take away; adding more "less?" Since adding is a feature of morality, we confuse ourselves and begin to believe that just because we are adding, we are still moral. This would explain why we say things like, "it feels so right, it can't be wrong." But adding less is still immoral. In chapter 7 we discussed how, since the 1960's, more and more, America's family structure has been becoming less and less. When immorality becomes the new morality and death becomes the new life, society is in trouble. This is why Scott Rae says morally neutral education will not work in our schools. What good is reading, writing and arithmetic if bad (life lessening activities) has become the new good and immorality has taken the place of morals?

In his book *Democracy Matters*, Cornell West rightly sees that when it comes to the future, young people "are so disillusioned because they can see that the adult world itself is so bereft of morality."[10] As I talk to young people and their young parents, many echo the words of Hip Hop star Jim Jones in his 2006 anthem, *Ballin'* where he warned, "Here today could be gone tomorrow, so I speed through life like there's no tomorrow." The irony is that his solution is full of the problem he is running from. Instead of creating speed bumps to slow down his life in the fast lane, he races and raises the speed limit, adding more immorality which only bumps up the mortality rate and shortens his life expectancy.

We cannot be an immoral society and expect our youth not to be morbid; they are the most honest reflection of our morals. In 2007, urban fashion designers catered to our cultural courtship with the casket as skulls became the most popular emblem on clothing in cities all across the country. When morality is low, mortality will be high. After all, (or before all, in the Garden of Eden) it was our immorality that brought on our mortality in the first place.

The Bible links immorality to mortality

The Bible's point is clear. In Proverbs chapter 8, God's Wisdom actually speaks for itself and says to mankind, "God made me before he made you." Wisdom says that it was not just created to govern mountains and oceans and animals, but kings and ordinary people just the same. As man was being made,

Wisdom was right there, delighting in these new human creatures and how morality would keep them on track. Then at the end of the poetic chapter, Wisdom warns, "All who hate me, love death." As much as we hate to hear it, the truth is, it is impossible to live without a source of mortality.

We have chosen immorality and have experienced death ever since. But God never uses the word immorality; instead, he uses words like sin, disobedience, unrighteousness, evil and wickedness. And he does not use the word mortality; he comes flat out and says, "Death." He told Adam and Eve they would die, and they eventually did. But even before they tasted physical death, they got to sample a soufflé of situations and relationships that were seasoned by death: blame shifting in their marriage and the murder of one of their sons by the other. In fact, there has not been a single moment since sin snuck onto the scene that our planet has not known animosity, war and death: man against God; man against wife; brother against brother; nation against nation; man against nature.

Yet all of this mortality, including physical death, is still only a portion of what God promised. In the Bible, we read that God actually adds another death on top of our physical mortality. This is what the Bible calls, "the second death" where the soul experiences separation from the divine-command-giver and judicial punishment for all immorality done while in the body.* The bad news from the beginning of this chapter just got worse. But if you remember, we also have good news to share which should make all the difference in the world.

Connecting the Dots to the Good News

We all, like Bruce Willis' *Sixth Sense* character, have been dead since the opening scene in Genesis 3. Like him, we have

---

* The Bible, Revelation 20:6

been terrorizing our children, unable to comfort mothers and disconnected from our loved ones. But the good news begins with this; God is not dead as we have supposed. We are the dead ones but God is alive. Our morbid minds must have mixed up the messages being sent by our senses. We have confused the ceasing of our obedience to God with causality for His casualty. Like the ultimate invisible friend, or perhaps *Beetle Juice*, we have told ourselves that God only exists as much as we believe in him. If we believe a little, He exists a little. If we believe very much, he is very much alive. And like Nietzsche, if we stop believing in God altogether, call the reverend and ready the hearse; he's a goner.

But it is the other way around. Our faith is a centrifugal force that works in reverse. The more we believe in God, the more *we* are alive, and the less we believe in him, the less we live. To say "God is Dead," is to pronounce our own death sentence. But there is hope.

Remember Russell Crowe, out to rescue Meg Ryan's kidnapped husband? The first thing he did before committing to the mission was to demand proof of life. He would not pay for it; he wanted it in "good faith." Well the God of the Bible does something very similar. He demands proof of life when he commits to rescuing us from our mortality. But he doesn't just demand it *in* good faith. The proof of life he wants from us *is* good faith because no good thing that immoral mortals can do is enough to make them moral again. Why not? Because even in their good, there is immorality: there is pride, there is self-righteousness, there are mixed motives, there is a side-stepping of the superlative, there is lack of trust in the deontological-command-giver. This has become our nature.

So, what's the good news? It begins with a miracle where God deposits *in* us the good faith that He demands *from* us, and then counts it as proof of life, proof of morality, or what the Bible calls righteousness.* This is how he revives immoral mortals, bringing them back to life; calling and causing them to live by faith in every area of morality that they once trusted themselves to figure out. They go on to live by this faith and by it, they even conquer death. In the Bible's book of Revelation, we are told that the faithful will not be hurt by the second death.† But the good news gets even better. It is not just "having faith," that counts. It is the Gospel, the thing that God calls us to put our good faith in that really matters.

The Gospel of Jesus Christ is this – the immorality of the faithful is not simply forgotten by God. It is judged and punished at the cross of Jesus Christ and they are forgiven by grace and through faith. And there's more, all of the righteousness, all of the *MORE*-ality of Jesus is then counted as belonging to those who believe. And because of his *MORE*-ality, mortality is no longer their fate. In the Gospel account written by John, Jesus is recorded as saying, "I am the resurrection and the life. Whoever believes in me, even though he dies, yet shall he live."‡ How was he able to promise this? Who was he? Was he God as Christians say? Or even the Son of God? And what do these chapters on philosophy and faith have to do with the previous chapters on fathers and family? If you are asking these questions then you are now ready for the most moral chapter of this book as we lift our eyes to behold The Moral Immortal.

---

* The Bible, Romans 4: 1-8
† The Bible, Revelation 20: 6
‡ The Bible, John 11: 25

Getting the Big Picture

1. Do you agree with the author that our world produces more proof of death than proof of life? Why or why not?

2. Do you see yourself as producing less and less or more and more quality of life for your world? Can you give examples?

3. Discuss "safe sex" according to the author.

4. At the beginning of this chapter, the author states that "unless some miracle has occurred you do not have more life left now than when you woke up this morning." At the end of the chapter he talks about a miracle where God deposits "good faith" in us. How does this change the outlook on life from "glass half empty" to "glass half full?"

13 The Moral Immortal

*A*fter examining the ways immorality has impacted our society, then suggesting that God is not dead as the humanists suppose, I can see no way forward except but to take a closer look at the person of God as found in the pages of the Bible. Everything before now has been said with a bit of a bitten tongue, but it is time to let the cat out of the bag (or better yet, the Lion out of the cage). In this short chapter we will look at five quick, quickening truths to explain why we must turn to face this God and what it is that qualifies Him as The Moral Immortal.

1. He Says the Most Moral Thing

In chapter 8, we saw the linguistic link between "father" and "author." Both words refer to "someone who has authority to prescribe, describe or inscribe instructions for increase and growth." In chapter 11 we concluded that the word "moral" also carries this same concept of causing more or adding to life. Thus, a father's job is to introduce *MORE*-ality to those under his care. In the pages of the Bible we see God, the Father, doing just that.

Throughout the New Testament, even though Jesus is portrayed as deity, we see him often praying to God in heaven and addressing him as "father." But why? What exactly is it that makes God "father?" First, Psalm 119 praises God as the Author of the prescribed, inscribed law; he is the deontological-command-giver. His commands are authoritative and they are life causing. Later, in the Bible's book of Acts, Jesus is called the "Author of Life" and John's Gospel account calls Jesus the Word of God who was *with* God in the beginning and *was* God. The Greek word used for "Word" here is a philosophical term - "logos," which means the symbolism of the highest idea or ideal.

Several verses later John says that, "The Word (logos) became flesh and dwelt among us." The Bible never says that Jesus was created but that he was "the Word" with God in the beginning. This means that there was never a point when God the father was without the expression of the highest ideal. If this is true, then it is Jesus who solidifies God's title as author-father since, by eternally uttering Jesus - the Author of Life, God the Father says, and has always been saying, the most moral Thing!

2. He made man in His moral image

Many have debated the meaning of God's words in Genesis, "Let us make man in our likeness and in our image." Clearly this means that we can look at mankind and see something that resembles or reflects the Creator. But what aspect of mankind is in God's "likeness" and "image?" And with what part of ourselves do we reflect God? Is it our physical bodies? Does the fact that we have two arms, two legs and two lips make us like God? Not likely, Scripture informs us that God is not dependant on a physical body.*

How about the fact that we possess the three main ingredients that are believed by some to make up personhood – intellect, will and emotion – does this make us like God? Possibly; but demons, even though they are not human, are persons. They have intellect (Satan schemes[†]); will (angels along with Satan chose to rebel against God[‡]); and emotion (demons tremble with fear at God's judgment[§]); and yet they are

---

* The Bible, John 4: 24
† The Bible, 2 Corinthians 2: 11
‡ The Bible, Jude 1: 6
§ The Bible, James 2: 19

are not said to be in the "image of God." The lack of God's image in them may explain why there is no record in the Bible of a divine mission to rescue fallen angels; only fallen man.

The "image" may have more to do with what Solomon said in the Biblical book Ecclesiastes, "God has placed eternity in the hearts of men."* He has given man a longing for lasting; for *MORE*-ality. God made man in His moral image and might as well have said on the sixth day, "let us make man moral." This is what man fell away from in Genesis 3. Our physical form was not altered. Our intellect, will and emotion still remain but are trapped in immorality because what was lost is our soul's map to morality.

Our purpose is wrapped up in reflecting. We were made to morally reflect God. This means we must turn to face him and behold him, otherwise we are reflecting nothing. A mirror cannot look within itself for an image to project; that would only produce emptiness of the most infinite kind. Battle rapper, Can-i-bus, once rapped, "Every word that I utter for Hip Hop lovers will reflect forever like two mirrors facing each other." This was one of the deepest, or as we say, "illest" rap lyrics ever at the time. If you've ever placed two mirrors in front of one another than you are familiar with the seemingly infinite images that result.

But there is a slight fallacy in this lyric. Two mirrors completely facing each will not produce an infinite reflection of anything at all. In order to get the 'endless mirrors' effect you must tilt at least one of the mirrors so as to pick up an image to reflect – be it the mirror's frame or something else in the room. For this reason, songs like Michael Jackson's *Man in the Mirror* are only able to produce minimum change. They fail to consider the fact that the man in the mirror *is* a mirror. And if he is not

---

* The Bible, Ecclesiastes 3: 11

reflecting anything but himself or another man-mirror, he is hollow. There must be something in view. God didn't just make us; he made us to be in his image. He is the moral One.

3. Good fathers reflect the Father

There are many good fathers in the world, many of whom do not consider themselves to be very religious. How did they get to be good and what are they reflecting? Knowingly or unknowingly, every good father must be tilted to some degree in order to pick up the moral image of the first father, God. Take a look at the Bible's 10 Commandments and notice the order in which they fall.* The first four commandments deal with our (vertical) relationship and response to God, the command giver. The last five deal with our (horizontal) social relationships with one another.

Right in the middle, however, is the 5th Commandment to honor your father and mother. It feels a bit funny to place it with the first four, and yet a little out of place with the last five. It sort of sits alone and operates on an angle, tilted not quite vertical and not quite horizontal. This is because it is through our parents that we first deal with God by honoring them as his representatives. The 5th Commandment operates as a hinge upon which we swing from dealing with God to dealing with man. This is why the 5th Commandment warns that if we do not honor our parent's instruction, which should be a reflection of God's instruction, we sabotage our own happiness.

Christian counselor Ed Welch suggests that in reality God is the original "husband, *the* father, *the* brother, and *the* friend."[1] With each of the biblical roles we see God in, he is not just telling us that he is *like* these things; rather that he *is* these things. By allowing us to play similar roles, Welch says, God is

---

* The Bible, Deuteronomy 5: 7-21

giving us "snapshots" of himself. The many different relationship roles we play are all just reflections of God and, "anything in the created world that bears a resemblance to these descriptions of God is simply God's glory spilling into creation and creatures. Whenever you see these, albeit distorted images [of God] in other people, they are a faint reflection of the original. I am a father because God is a father." And a good father gives good morals to his child, not just horizontally (how to deal with man), but vertically (how to deal with God). The best fathers are tilted; angled so that they can both catch and cast God's moral image. The best fathers, reflect The Father.

4. He judges immorality

In chapter 12 we discussed mankind's "death reflex," and how we naturally look to bring an end to things that strike us as immoral. This instinct is simply a dim reflection of our moral Maker; it is something we get from a moral God. People who choose not to subscribe to any organized religion but say they 'believe in God and that God is good' are faced with a dilemma – what does a good God do about immorality or evil? When thinking of the problem of the existence of evil, St. Augustine finally rested in the realization that evil is not a thing that actually exists. Anything that exists, he reasoned, must be good to some degree or else it would not exist at all. Evil, then, is simply the process by which that which is moral becomes less and less good until it can no longer exist.[2] And sin is any desire for or action toward evil ends.

Immorality decreases and destroys things until death reigns, but morality plots, plans and produces life of the everlasting type. So what does morality do when it meets immorality? Or better yet, what does the Moral Immortal do when he meets immoral mortals? The answer is built right into the question. Immoral mortals are only mortal because the Moral Immortal will not allow them to have unending life in their immoral state. Selah.* In fact, to allow immorality forever is an oxymoron; it would be like allowing something to become less and less, forever and ever. But God does not permit this in his presence. He judges immorality. It would be impossible to consider him good or moral were he to let it go unchecked.

God's plan to deal with immorality can be compared to the building and collapse of the World Trade Center in 2001. On the infamous date of 9/11, the unthinkable happened. When hijackers flew two planes into the Twin Towers in New York city, nearly 2800 lives were lost as both buildings came tumbling down in a cloud of glass, metal and debris. But there was a blessing even in this catastrophe. The destruction would have been even greater had the builders of those towers not planned for the worst. It is a testimony to the wisdom and morality of the builders that the blueprints included a design for disaster; a safety feature in case the towers ever had to come down. The design was for the towers, if need be, to collapse upon themselves instead of tilting and toppling over upon neighboring buildings.

Our moral Maker has constructed mankind in a similar way. The more immoral we are, the faster, or else harder, we fall. However, any damage we happen to cause throughout the course of our lives would be far worse if God had not built us in such a way that we eventually collapse upon our own immoral selves and can then do no more harm. We cannot go on being immoral forever. In Genesis chapter 5, we read about people living as long as 969 years and then dying. But in chapter 6 God announces that he will limit man's life to only 120 years. This reduction of life-span came as God looked at the wickedness of man and exclaimed, "My Spirit will not always morally compete with man."† God had already installed the deadly device due to

---

* Selah = Take a moment to reflect on this statement
† The Bible, Genesis 6:3; Author's paraphrase

Adam's disobedience but he adjusted the alarming clock of death so that we would have just enough time to live, become convinced of our need for him and perhaps find him, but not live so long that we might forget that we were mortal and cause unlimited damage with our unlimited years.*

In fact, he has rigged it so that no matter where we look in this life, we can never forget about death because the whole universe has gotten in on the act. In the play, *As You Like It*, Shakespeare popularized the phrase, "All the world's a stage, and all the men and women are merely actors." But what if our "stage" is not a fan of our performance? Suppose the "stage" has even been set to synchronize with our sinful scenes? In the New Testament book of Romans, the Apostle Paul writes that the entire universe is groaning and crumbling in upon itself as a direct result of mankind's sin.† In his classic sermon, *Sinners in the Hands of an Angry God*, Jonathon Edwards shouts that, "if it were not for the sovereign pleasure of God" to keep you here for the time being:

> The earth would not bear you [for] one moment; for you are a burden to it. The creation groans [because of] you....The sun don't willingly shine upon you to give you light to serve sin and Satan. The earth don't willingly yield her increase to satisfy your lusts; nor is it willingly a stage for your wickedness to be acted upon. The air don't willingly serve you for breath to maintain the flame of life in your vitals, while you spend your life in the service of God's enemies. God's [creations] are good, and made for men to serve God with, and [they] don't willing serve any other purpose, and groan when they are abused to [serve] purposes so directly contrary to their nature and end.3

It has often been asked, 'why do bad things happen to

---

* The Bible, Acts 17: 26,27
† The Bible, Romans 8: 19-22

good people and why do good things happen to bad people? If God wanted to be seen as the most moral, he should only let bad things happen to bad people.' But as we saw in chapter 11, our opinion of what makes a good or bad person can be extremely handicapped by our inability to measure the extent of a person's good or bad deeds. Therefore, when someone dies, no matter how they leave this world, be it a nasty car accident or natural catastrophe, before we allege that God is not good we must remember that people do not belong to this earth, they belong to God. The Bible tells us that at death, the body returns to the earth from which it came, but the spirit returns to the Lord who gave it.* And also, "it is appointed to each person once to die, and after that, the real judgment."†

5. Even His death brings life

Picture a tombstone; better yet, picture your tombstone. It will have two dates on it, separated by a dash. The dash, as Christian rapper Tonic says, represents your life. The first date you already know – your birth-date; the second date will speak for itself sooner or later. God has already told us that the span between those two dates will not be longer than 120 years. But what about God? What would God's tombstone say? Nietzsche supposed the second date on God's tombstone to be somewhere in the 1800's. The Bible gives God a different set of dates. Psalm 90 says of the LORD, "From everlasting to everlasting, You are God." Which sort of sounds like "no beginning and no end." For God, there is not a dash in the middle of two dates. The first date for him is a dash with an arrow going to the left. The second date for him is another dash with an arrow going in the opposite direction. And the dashes just keep on going. The Biblical prophet Isaiah says God is the "High and Lofty One who inhabits

---

* The Bible, Ecclesiastes 12:7
† The Bible, Hebrews 9: 27

eternity."*

God lives forever. That makes him immortal. But what if he were immortal, and yet not very moral; always living to destroy something? Who could stop him? A classic Christian cliché volleys the phrase, "God is good, all the time; and all the time, God is good." What is sometimes meant by this is 'God is good to *me*.' But this fails to acknowledge that even if God were not being particularly good to me, he would still be good. Why? Because God is not trying to perform up to some separate standard of goodness that is located somewhere outside of himself, in our opinions or elsewhere in the universe. Not at all. "Good" has always had to wait on God to see what he has purposed in order to get a proper definition of its self. Not only does "good" not know its self unless God purposes, but we too are clueless as to what "good" is if God does not consciously or subconsciously orient us in us his goals. The Bible announces that God does whatever he pleases and yet all His acts are just.†
‡

For some that is a scary thought. "It could just as well please him to do something evil," they fear. The only safety is in God's nature, which assures us that even if something seems evil to us, if God has chosen to do it, it is good. In his classic work, *The Knowledge of the Holy*, A.W. Tozer wrote that in the Bible:

> "Wisdom, when used of God and good men, always carries a strong moral connotation....Wisdom...is the ability to devise perfect ends and to achieve those ends by the most perfect means....All God's acts are done in perfect wisdom, first for His own glory, and then for the highest good of the greatest number for the longest time."[4]

In The Chronicles of Narnia, C.S. Lewis writes of Aslan

* The Bible, Isaiah 57: 15
† The Bible, Psalm 135: 6
‡ The Bible, Psalm 145:17

the Lion, who's character is Christ, "'course he isn't safe, but he's good!"[5] *What* he is makes him unsafe; *how* he is, or rather *Who* he is, is our only security. God is not like the "Energon cube" from the popular *Transformer* movies, shooting raw energy everywhere, transforming lifeless objects into living machines, which come to life armed and dangerous and even evil. That cube, though it gives life, is not moral. God is! Every square in God's cube is completely filled with *MORE*-ality.

But if Christians believe that God is both moral and immortal, how can they say that Jesus is God and still believe that he died on the cross for the sins of the world? There is a most moral answer to this. On a mission to take the second death away from immoral mortals, the Moral Immortal has done something spectacular. The Moral Immortal became mortal - killable. But, since the only way to be mortal is to be attached to immorality, the Moral Immortal had to adopt someone's sin. Referring to Jesus, the Bible says that "*he* who knew no sin, became sin for us."[*] And that God the father "has placed on *him* the [immorality] of us all," and at that point, "it pleased the LORD to crush *him*" because "the punishment that would bring us peace was upon *him*."[†]

But it gets even more moral. The scriptures say that God the father vindicated Jesus, clearing his good name by raising him from the dead since he had no immorality of his own for which he should have to die.[‡] Jesus was so supremely moral and and his death such a severe moral injustice, that releasing him from the grave instantly produced immortality for untold numbers of past, present and future souls who looked forward, looked to or look back upon him by faith. I would close by

---

[*] The Bible, 2nd Corinthians 5: 21
[†] The Bible, Isaiah 53: 5
[‡] The Bible, 1 Timothy 3: 16

saying, "It doesn't get any more moral than that," but that would not be true. This is only the beginning of *MORE*-ality.

If this is not your faith, I encourage you to investigate and incorporate a strong source of morality for your future. Our culture will not offer you one and yet this is the one thing that will save up from anarchy. In the final chapter, I invite you to become a part of the movement - Beyond Positivity.

Getting the Big Picture

1. Which is more important, that God is Moral or that he is Immortal, or are they of equal importance? Explain your answer.

2. Do you see God more as Father, as God, equally the same or as neither?

3. How does the author's explanation of God as Father impact your understanding of God's role in your life?

4. What can fathers today learn from this description of God as father?

14 Beyond Positivity

"*I*f your kids put you through even half the hell you put me through, you'll be back here apologizing on your hands and knees." Those words end up on the lips or the tip of the tongue of just about every mother at some point during the parenting years. Apparently, those parents who raised the first generation of Hip Hopped tots are now ready to induct their grown children into this ironic "I told you so" hall of fame. If you listen, you can hear the distressing cry from Generation X'ers back to their parents as they confess, "You were right!" Moms in their late 20's and mid-30's find themselves back in the kitchen, humbled beside their gloriously graying mothers, trying to soak up the wisdom they once sidestepped. Young fathers find themselves frantically pacing, piecing together a version of manhood in order to have something to show their sons.

It is all too obvious that today's parents are still too young to play their proper role; not young in age, but in stage of life and state of mind. Because of this youthful yoke, the growth of the urban family tree has been radically retarded. In the 70's and 80's fathers were divorcing mothers and leaving the home in record numbers. In the 90's many fathers were never even in the home to begin with. Now in the new millennium, many youth are growing up in homes where neither mom nor dad is a resident. Foster care, and foster care abuse is a common experience. But this is what Arnold J. Gibbs was warning against when he objected to the No Fault Divorce Law. This is what Maggie Gallagher foresaw as she warned against a society where marriage was no longer the norm. We should have expected that the loss of family and the exaltation of the individual, fueled by post-modern, egoistic ethics would produce such personal confusion and cultural chaos.

Solutions anyone?

Perhaps America may want to consider doing what the Romans Empire did when they wanted to reform their failing immoral society. They understood the importance of family and aimed to make marriage more attractive by offering tax breaks to the married and putting higher taxes on single men. But, we already have something like this. That will not be enough as long as the backdoor of No Fault Divorce is still propped open. Maybe we should look into making marriage harder to come by; mandatory premarital counseling or some other kind of accountability.

I am not a Politian and do not understand the complexities involved in making laws. But there is one thing I do know. America created these young minded adults by inventing "teenagers." If "teenager" is defined by an endless list of "can'ts:" can't smoke, can't drink, can't drive, can't marry, can't work...etc. and no one is informing our youth of all of their "can do's" or "should do's," then they will remain "ability with no responsibility" well into their adult lives. In contrast, educator Dorothy Sayers marveled at the "remarkably early age at which the young men went up to university," and matured in the sixteenth century. In an essay arguing for a return to Classical education she wrote, that:

> if we are to produce a society of educated people, fitted to preserve their intellectual freedom amid the complex pressures of our modern society, we must turn back the wheel of progress some four or five hundred years, to the point at which education began to lose sight of its true object, towards the end of the Middle Ages.[1]

Perhaps we need a new approach to education that goes beyond the three "R's". Sayers believed that instead of teaching students disconnected "subjects" we should be, as they were in the Middle Ages, teaching people to learn, reason, and integrate the world's knowledge. She criticized the fact that we teach people to read just enough to become victims to the "influence of advertisement and mass propaganda." Think of the smutty "urban novels" written at a fourth grade reading level that attract so many of our teen and pre-teen girls. Sayers argued that young men and women are being sent out to fight these influences with only a "smattering of subjects [while] whole classes and whole nations become hypnotized by the arts of the spell binder; and we have the [nerve] to be astonished," like Steve Perry in the opening chapter.

Based on the model of Aristotle, Classical Learning focuses on three areas. The first is *Grammar* (the basic tools for each future subject) taught from ages 4 to 11. Like in the Middle Ages, Sayers recommends learning Latin or Greek, partly for the useful linguistic building blocks contained in each but also because the literary history of the Ancient world has largely been translated into one of these two languages. Secondly, *Dialectic*, which includes logic and the art of disputation, she suggests for ages 12 to 14. "The debating subjects of the Middle Ages were drawn largely from theology or from the ethics and history of antiquity." As we have stated, this is not simply for mental discipline, but for forging moral fortitude.

Theology was once called the Queen of the sciences; it has now been reduced to what Sayers calls the "mistress of science." But if children are properly educated, it should lead them to asking thoughtful questions about the world, history and the here-after, origin and destiny. The disconnectedness of education from life and ultimate reality is part of what is ailing this generation. The third area, *Rhetoric*, consists of intelligently and elegantly expressing one's own thoughts. This covers ages 15 and 16. After this point it is on to trade school or higher learning as each one's path demands. This is very similar to the education process Du Bois favored. Sayers believed that:

At the end of the Dialectic [stage], the children will probably seem to be far behind [those] brought up on old-fashioned "modern" methods, so far as detailed knowledge of specific subjects is concerned. But after the age of 14 they should be able to overhaul the others hand over fist....[And] get the mastery of a new subject in half the time and with a quarter of the effort expended by the person who [does not have these] tools at his command.

A solution to the solution

If we will not or cannot change our education model then there is one thing that we can and must do – inject daily, culturally relevant, character education into our schools. After a three month break from teaching the character courses I helped to develop with Philadelphia's Urban Family Council, I returned to Olney High School to visit with students and teachers. When asked how things were going, Mrs. Hayes, the special ed. teacher responded, "The inmates run the jail! Until we deal with the real issues going on at home, nothing *here* will change." School is the one place that children cannot escape for long and if ethical training is no longer coming from the home, it behooves us to take advantage of this daily opportunity to instill this content.

Several challenges prevent this from happening on a large scale. One thing is that students must pass standardized yearly progress exams and to do this, teachers must teach at an impossible pace for most inner-city schools. To free up time for daily character education would only further frustrate this task. One solution could be to loosen the slack on the testing, especially since some schools are already resorting to forging test results that really do not reflect the true failure rate of their student body. If more time were spent on character education, more students might actually pass these standardized tests.

Another challenge might be that "culturally relevant,

character education" seems like a fairy tale; a dream that will never come true. Either the curriculum or the communicators of it will fail to be relevant to urban youth. But this is important. Professor Joseph L. White (PHD.) advised that we need role models in the classroom that look like students, "as opposed to role models that look like what the students 'should want to' look like." In June of 2010, President Obama and U.S. Secretary of Education, Arne Duncan announced an initiative to increase the number of black male teachers across America. Until that happens, Professor White suggests that we go to:

> Our colleges and universities. Have Black male undergraduate students in the [public school]. Bring them in as hall monitors; have them present in the environment in multiple ways, as coaches, tutors, mentors; use them in meaningful roles. Give these students real training as black male role models; don't just dump them in.[2]

But having been in the inner-city school system, I know that it is difficult to find young men who can connect with the younger generation but who also happen to have the morals and values needed to properly combat rather than contribute to the social problems of the city. However, there is a beautiful solution to this challenge which I pray we are ready for.

The Name Game

Where could we possibly find an army of mentors relevant enough to reach today's youth, and reliable enough to relay the right information? As it turns out, since many urban youth and their parents share the same culture and values, it is just as necessary to reach out to the parents of today's youth, and there is a contingent of people who are just right for the job. They can be found in the most unlikely place. There is still one fruitful branch extending from Hip Hop's tree that we have yet to examine. I have saved this group for last because it is perhaps this group that may at last, save us. They have already recovered the dropped baton and began to run with it; only the news cameras have not focused our attention on them just yet. Therefore I will close by introducing this new breed and illustrating why we should support and celebrate them as the rightful recipients of the baton from the historical hand of the Civil Rights generation.

In the third chapter we made a distinction between Conscious rap and Positive rap, suggesting that while conscious rappers are known for their attempts to keep the culture socially sober, Positive rap is more known for its efforts to erase overly negative content. If the rapper does not curse (much); does not endorse drug-use or drug-dealing; does not objectify women – we typically refer to their music as positive. But this may not be the case. When discussing morality in chapter 11 we stated that "Just chillin'" is an inadequate answer to the question, "What's really good?" because someone who is always just chilling is not being about the business of morality.

In the same way, just because some rap music contains no negatives does not automatically mean that it is positive. To be truly positive it must go beyond just chilling and move us forward in the direction of what *should* be. If something is neither negative nor positive, it does no harm but it also does no good. And as we have said, doing no good counts as immorality. But since rap that aims to be morally neutral already gets credit for being positive, we will label our final group Beyond Positivity.

I have had the honor and pleasure of being a part of this movement Beyond Positivity for over sixteen years and wholeheartedly believe that it is this movement that will finally guide the current generation back on track. This movement has gone by different names and through different stages throughout its young history. We have looked at "Street-hop" and observed the more edgy "Strip-hop," we will now peer into what may be termed "Script-hop."

I became a Christian in 1992. Though still in high school, it was a year of solitude. Later that year I met a young man on a similar path. This youngster was not only serious about his faith, he was vocal about it. For most young people, faith is foreign. But he was vocal in a very familiar way. "I rap for the Lord," he said. This was the first time I'd ever considered the possibility of merging my faith and my culture. Why had no one ever told me this was possible? And what would be the result if I tried? What followed was dynamic! It felt as if my faith was on steroids; or was it my culture on steroids? Either way I was stronger in both circles when I no longer had to zip off my culture to put on my faith or vice-versa. We formed a rap group and a year later met others who had been doing the same.

Faith plus culture; we were Christians rapping, but what do you call that? Is it Christian rap? Christian Hip Hop? Holy Hip Hop? Gospel rap? The Dove and Grammy award shows still have a hard time naming, let alone respecting the category. There has even been "in-house" debate as to whether the term "Christian" needs to be attached to the title at all. We were on the East Coast. But across the country there had already been a host of MCs who approached the subject in reverse; not Christians rapping, but rappers who happen to be Christians. There is a slight difference. Rappers who just happened to be Christians may or may not feel the need to be vocal concerning their faith, whereas the Christian who just happens to rap is more prone to poetic proclamations of faith.

It turns out this difference in ideology may be more a difference in stage of entrance. Often, the stage in which one enters Hip Hop determines how they use it? It is interesting that for just about every Hip Hop stage, Christians can be seen standing mirror to mirror alongside the culture attempting to reflect *MORE*-ality into it – unfortunately, sometimes we did a better job at catching the culture's image than casting a moral image into it.

For Hip Hop's Battle stage, the Christian rapper entered the cipher through groups such as the Tunnel Rats. When secular rap was dominated by the gangster rapper, the Christian too was a gangster, only he was doing drive-bys on demons. Artists who entered and entertained on this stage include T-Bone and the Original Gospel Gangstaz. Where secular rap was concerned with knowledge of self and Edutainment, the Christian rapper was entertaining and educating his listener about self from God's perspective and about God's self. Artists who mirrored this version of Hip Hop include The Cross Movement and Lamp Mode Record's Shai Linne and Stephen the Levite. Secular rap has had a partying side with a commercial flare and so has the Christian rap arena in the careers of The Grits and KJ 52. When secular rap became synonymous with "blingin" and "ballin," the Christian rapper also began to floss godliness as a way to "come up." In BB J's *Don't Be Mad* he bragged that it was because of Jesus that he and his team were "stackin paper," "laced in ice" and driving awesome automobiles.

I speak from other's testimony and not my own testosterone when I say that The Cross Movement has had a most lasting impact on the world of Christian Hip Hop. This is partly because the members of the group spanned 10 years in age and had each entered Hip Hop during different stages of the culture's evolution. This enabled us to present a variety of the culture's traits on one collective platter. Many also say the group's legacy is due to a commitment to sound Biblical teaching through our lyrics. Aside from helping a host of northeast artists produce and release albums, The Cross Movement has also lent steam to and helped launch artists who stylistically mirror Hip Hop's journey to the Midwest and South by signing and co-signing releases from rappers Flame, Lacrae and K-Drama. Across the country and around the world, countless others have taken up the enterprise of blending their faith and culture – too many to name in this book, but they rejoice that their names are written in another.*

Un-commissioned Missionaries

What is it that qualifies this faith and culture blending brigade to carry the baton? First, they speak the language of today's generation and possibly tomorrow's since yesterday and today's youth culture are one and the same. Christian Hip Hopped individuals are indigenous to this culture and climate and if anyone were to be sent in as a humanitarian missionary, they are the most likely candidates. Second, the Christian Hip Hopped individual, unlike many who are not of the faith, share much of the values of the Civil Rights generation. They value education and higher education. They are peace makers, even in this violent world. Even with all of their newness they embrace the "old morality" of monogamous marriage and sexual purity. And, if they fail at this, they believe they should be removed from their platform until they are morally corrected, as was evidenced in 2009 when Cross Movement Records would not endorse two of its marquee artists who were found to be unfaithful in marriage.

Frederick Nietzsche, Bertrand Russell and Victoria Woodhull all called for a new morality concerning marriage and sex. But instead of a new morality, Christian's believe that God is giving something better, new hearts. The Biblical prophet Ezckicl hears God announcing that one day God will put a new heart in his people and cause them to walk according to statutes.† Our Christian Hip Hopped heroes in training are entering that "day."

They are not perfect. Though grown, many are socially

---

* The Bible, Luke 10: 20
† The Bible, Ezekiel 36: 26, 27

still teenagers in many ways. Almost everyone born after the 1960's is. But they are the best teenagers we have and are learning to leave their teenaged ways behind. However, they are un-commissioned. They are idle. Like the children of the 40's and 50's who were forced from their jobs. They are not trusted to hold many posts because of their youthful ways (or looks). But we have already seen what idleness produces in the hands of a youthful generation. Somehow they must be trusted or tried, and even then they must be trained. Because eventually, soon, the current posts will have to be handed down and someone must be ready to take over. And who better?

After the Music Stops

In 2007, Christian rapper Lacrae released the album *After the Music Stops*. The theme communicates our final thought and can be carried even farther. One key concern for the Christian rapper is that, just like with secular rap, the mission of reaching the people can be easily abandoned when the opportunity for commercial success arises. This is likely the reason that the Moral Immortal has allowed success to elude the genre as a whole. In 2005, Christian and secular artists alike begin to realize there was a hole in the bottom of the music industry's money bag; two holes in fact, torn by the same tool – technology. The holes were: access to digital downloading and an excess of digital uploading as discussed in chapter 10.

All of this was perhaps a blessing in disguise. Like the men at the tower of Babel who were forced to spread out and get back on the mission of *MORE*-ality when their languages were confused; or the early church which was forced to get back on the Great Commission due to Roman persecution; the movement to go Beyond Positivity may also be advanced by the frustration of our capitalistic aims and attempts at celebrity. We are being pushed out to pursue more moral goals and roles.

Adam's job was *MORE*-ality; adding to. For the Christian Hip Hopped individual, there are many ways to add; many places his or her gifts, skill set and cultural sensitivities can be useful – in classrooms as professors; on corners as police; in congress as politicians; in churches as pastors. Those who do not rap are forced to play some of these other positions. But even the rapper may find that the people he or she claims to be concerned about reaching will be more accessible, more touchable, and more changeable as we exit the stage and begin to explore more practical, incarnational forms of ministry. Christian Hip Hop has a chance to grow in ways that secular Hip Hop has not. So far, we have not yet seen an adult version of Christian Hip Hop and the musical aspect is still looked at as youth ministry. The church is still set up for and in stride with the previous movement. But growing socially, off the stage and outside of the studio will effectively allow this counter-culture to grow up and win the blessing and commission of Runner #1.

If more moral agents from this community are not motivated and commissioned to enter the broader scope of society soon, not only will we miss an opportunity for maximum impact, but we may eventually see the same kind of cultural death among Christian Hip Hop as Nas eulogized for the broader culture. There may continue to be more concerts, downloads, T-shirts, message boards and mixtapes, but all this "more" will only produce less. If you listen, you might even hear the music fading. Listen carefully and you might hear the pen scratching the page. If you look hard, you might even see the handwriting on the wall from Hip Hop's next "Dear John" dedication, this time to Script-hop, which might read something like this:

Dear John (Wells),

---

* John Wells is CEO of Cross Movement Records, one of the most trusted names in Christian Hip Hop.

Thank you for giving me a chance to do what I've always dreamed of – uplifting a people. We've been together for almost twenty years and just look at what we've accomplished. We created a counter-culture, a whole movement focused on souls instead of sales. We've had some great times running with the baton but I know that sooner or later you'll have to pass it to another generation. They are reaching for it even now. Before you release it into their grasp, make sure that they have a strong grip on the importance of maintaining culture, preserving family and most importantly, where they must turn for moral authority. Because without these, they will surely drop the baton; history will repeat itself; and I will go back to where I came from...you always said I was a gift from God.

One Love,

Hip Hop

Bibliography

Chapter ONE

[1] Steve Perry; Interview; CNN's Anderson Cooper 360; Aired October 27, 2009

[2] Benjamin T. Jealous; http://www.washingtonpost.com/wpdyn/content/article/200 9/ 07/11/AR2009071102466_2.html (posted July 12, 2009)

[3] Michael Eric Dyson; *April 4, 1968* (New York: Civitas 2008)

[4] Ibid

[5] Jeff Change; *Can't Stop, Won't Stop* (New York: Picador 2005) p. 45

[6] Abraham Maslow; *Towards a Psychology of Being*; (New York: Norstrand 1968) p. 21-35

Chapter THREE

[1] Meyer Weinberg; *W.E.B. Dubois: A Reader* (New Yorkr: Harper 1970) p. 111

[2] Heather Cox Richardson; *The Death of Reconstruction* (Cambridge: Harvard 2001) p. 216

[3] Ibid p. 196

[4] Ibid p. 221

[5] Philip G. Altbach, Berdahl, Robert O.; Gumport, Patricia J.; *American Higher Education in the Twenty-First Century* (Baltimore: Hopkins 2005) p. 48

[6] Ibid p. 40

[7] Ibid p. 41

[8] Ibid p. 45

[9] Christopher J. Lucas; *American Higher Education: A History* (New York: Griffin 1994) p. 144

[10] Heather Cox Richardson; *The Death of Reconstruction* (Cambridge: Harvard 2001) p. 217

[11] Hugh Hawkins; *Booker T. Washing and His Critics: The problem of Negro Leadership* (D.C.: Heath 1966) Intro. VI

[12] August Meier; *Negro Thought in America 1880 -1915: Racial Ideologies in age of Washington* (Michigan: Michigan 1964) p. 220 – 27

[13] W.E.B. Du Bois; *The Souls of Black Folk* (New York: Gramercy 1994) p. 40

[14] Meyer Weinberg; *W.E.B. Du Bois: A Reader* (New York: Harper 1970) p. 65

[15] Ibid 148

[16] Ibid 43

[17] W.E.B. Du Bois; *Dusk of Dawn*; (New York: Schocken 1968)

[18] Grace Elizabeth Hale; *Making Whiteness* (New York : Pantheon 1998) p. 21

[19] Meyer Weinberg; *W.E.B. Du Bois: A Reader* (New York: Harper 1970) p. 43

[20.] Ibid p. 77

[21] W.E.B. Du Bois; *The Souls of Black Folk* (New York: Gramercy 1994) p. 148

[22] Meyer Weinberg; *W.E.B. Du Bois: A Reader* (New York: Harper 1970) p. 159 – 60

[23] Booker T. Washington; *Up From Slavery* (New York: Barnes 2003) p. 76

[24.] Meyer Weinberg; *W.E.B. Du Bois: A Reader* (New York: Harper 1970) p. 21

[25] Ibid p. 8

[26] Kennedy Randall; *Nigger: The Strange Career of a Troublesome Word* (New York: Vintage 2003) p. 8

[27] Meyer Weinberg; *W.E.B. Du Bois: A Reader* (New York: Harper 1970) p. 7

[28] Jay Z; Interview. *Jay Z responds to T-Pain Diss!! Oh! Boy!!!*; http://www.youtube.com/watch?v=T6DI6b2AD8s; (September 8, 2009)

[29] Meyer Weinberg; *W.E.B. Du Bois: A Reader* (New York: Harper 1970) p. 219 – 20

[30] Ibid Intro. XV

[31] Ibid p. 436

Chapter FOUR

[1] Waka Flock Flame; Interview; *Waka Flocka Flame on Lyrics*; http://worldstarhiphop.com/videos/video800.php?v=wshh4HJ Y74MhNMER1Au1&set_size=1 (Feb. 26, 2010)

[2] Nas; Documentary; *And You Don't Stop*: 30 Years of Hip Hop (2004)

[3] Julie Landsman, Chance W. Lewis; *White Teachers Diverse Classrooms* (New York: Stylus 2006) p. 95

[4] Ibid. p. 95

[5] Secretary of Education, Arne Duncan; Interview; Telecast on CNN; Aired June 22, 2010

[6] NASFAA.org; October 14th 2003; Accessed November 15th; 2008;.http://www.nasfaa.org/publications/2003/rnminorityre port101403.html

[7] Young Jeezy, Monie Love; Interview; Dec 2006; Accessed June 11, 2009; http://www.youtube.com/watch?v=NIsL_VMCLwA;

Chapter FIVE

[1] Ghostface Killah; Online Article; *Ghostface Killah Upset with Fans Over Sales*; January 23, 2008; accessed 12/20/09 http://www.hiphop-elements.com/article/read/4/14539/1/

[2] The Smoking Gun; *Akon's Con Job*; accessed 12/20/09; http://www.hiphop-elements.com/article/read/4/14539/1/

[3] Charles Aaron; Online Article; *Could Hip Hop heal America's Racial Divide?*; May/June 1999; Accessed May 8, 2009 http://www.utne.com/1999-05-01/black-like-them.aspx?page=2

Chapter SIX

[1] http://www.merriam-webster.com/dictionary/teenage

[2] Allen Harris; Brett Harris; *Do Hard Things*; (Colorado: Multnomah 2008) p. 30

[3] Susan Campbell Bartoletti; *Kid's On Strike* (Boston: Houghton 1999) p. 10

[4] Ibid p. 24

[5] Milton Meltzer; *Cheap Raw Material* (New York: Viking 1994) p. 29

[6] Ibid p. 33

[7] Susan Campbell Bartoletti; *Kid's On Strike* (Boston: Houghton 1999) p. 41

[8] *Child Workers on City Streets*; U.S. Publication 160; 1928 p. 2

[9] Ibid p. 31

[10] US Department of Labor: Children's Bureau; *Advising Children* Pub. #53; April 6, 1918

[11] Susan Campbell Bartoletti; *Kid's On Strike* (Boston: Houghton 1999) p. 24

[12] Milton Meltzer; *Cheap Raw Material* (New York: Viking 1994) p. 72

[13] Ibid p. 80

[14] Thomas Harris; *I'm OK--You're OK* (New York: Harper 1969) p.28

[15] Joel Selvin; *Summer of Love*; Documentary Transcript; posted 3/14/07; accessed 6/17/09 http://www.pbs.org/wgbh /amex / love/filmmore/pt.html

[16] Time Magazine Article; *Youth: The Hippies*; First published July 7, 1967; Accessed June 23, 2010; http://www.time.com/time/ magazine /article/0,9171,899555-10,00.html

[17] Mary Kasper: *Summer of Love*; Documentary Transcript; posted 3/14/07; accessed 6/17/09 http://www.pbs.org/wgbh /amex / love/filmmore/pt.html

Chapter SEVEN

[1] Steven Levine; *Summer of Love*; Documentary Transcript; posted 3/14/07; accessed 6/17/09 http://www.pbs.org/wgbh /amex/love/filmmore/pt.html

[2] Ibid (Phil Morningstar)

[3] Victoria C. Woodhull; Speech; *And the Truth Shall Make You Free* (Delivered November 20, 1871)

[4] James T. Sears; *Greenwood Encyclopedia of Love, Courtship & Sexuality* (Westport: Greenwood 2008) p. 94

[5] Ibid p. 95

[6] Summer of Love; Documentary Transcript; posted 3/14/07; accessed 6/17/09 http://www.pbs.org/wgbh/amex/ love/ filmmore/pt.html

[7] David B. Brinkerhoff, Lynn K. White, Suzanne T. Ortega, Rose Weitz; *Essentials of Sociology* (Wadsworth 2005) p. 126 – 27

[8] Gilbert Osofsky; Harlem: *The Making of a Ghetto* (Chicago: Dee 1996) p. 149

[9] Grace Elizabeth Hale, *Making Whiteness* (New York: Pantheon 1998) p. 16

[10] Ira Berlin; *Slaves Without Masters* (New York: Vintage 1974) p. 60 - 61

[11] National Urban League; *The State of Black America: Portrait of the Black Male* (Silver Springs: Beckham 2007) p. 59

[12] Arnold J. Gibbs; American Bar Association Section of Family Law Recommendation; February 1974; Accessed 2008-08-12; http://www.uniformdivorce.com/Report-Read.pdf.

[13] Marry Gallagher; *The Abolition of Marriage* (D.C.: Regnery 1996) p.   9

[14] Ibid p. 4

[15] Ibid p.5

[16] Ibid p. 117

[17] Michael Eric Dyson; *April 4, 1968* (New York: Civitas 2008) p. 106

[18] Yahoo.com; Article; Accessed June 25, 2009; http://news. yahoo.com/s/ap/20090619/ap_on_go_pr_wh/us_obama_father hood

[19] CNN.com; Accessed February 12, 2009;http://www.cnn. com /2008/ LIVING/ personal/04/15/fragmented.families.ap/ index. html?iref=newsearch _blank

[20] Marry Gallagher; *The Abolition of Marriage* (D.C.: Regnery 1996) p. 48

[21] Life Site News; July 6, 2006; Accessed Jan 1, 2010; http://www.lifesitenews.com/ldn/2009/jul/09070603.html

[22] Marry Gallagher; *The Abolition of Marriage* (D.C.: Regnery 1996) p. 42

[23] Scott B. Rae; *Moral Choices* 2nd Edition (Grand Rapids: Zondervan 2000) p. 124

[24] *Abstinence 101* 6TH Edition; Sioux Falls 2007   p. 25

[25] James T. Sears; *Greenwood encyclopedia of Love, Courtship & Sexuality* (Westport: Greenwood 2008) p. 240

[26] W. E. B. Du Bois; *Black Folk and Birth Control*; Birth Control Review 16 (June 1932) p. 166-67

[27] Meyer Weinberg; W.E.B. Du Bois: A Reader (New York: Harper 1970) p. 148

[28] Abstinence 101 6TH Edition; Sioux Falls 2007   p. 25

[29] Kaiser Family Foundation; *Sex On TV 4*; November 2005; accessed November 2008; http://www.kff.org/entmedia/u pload/Sex-on-TV-4-Full-Report.pdf

[30] C.S. Lewis, *Mere Christianity*(San Francisco: Harper 1952)p. 99

Chapter EIGHT

[1] Jay Z; Online Article; Posted July 20, 2009;
http://www.sohh.com/2009/07/jay-z_says_age_is_just_a.html

[2] Lil Wayne; Interview; Accessed April 25, 2009;
http://www.youtube.com/watch?v=lyI26E5agM4

[3] http://hellobeautiful.com/your-world/mary-js-stepdaughter-puts-dad-on-blast/ (posted June 23, 2009)

[4] Marry Gallagher; *The Abolition of Marriage* (D.C.: Regnery 1996) p. 15

[5] David Blankenhorn; *Fatherless America* (New York: Harper 1995) p. 157

[6] Marry Gallagher; *The Abolition of Marriage* (D.C.: Regnery 1996) p. 67

[7] David Blankenhorn; *Fatherless America* (New York: Harper 1995) p. 154

[8]http://www.etymonline.com/index.php?search=author&searchmode=none (Accessed May 15, 2010)

[9] Yahoo.com; Article. Accessed June 31, 2009;
http://news.yahoo.com/s/ap/20090620/ap_on_go_pr_wh/us_obama_fatherhood

[10] Marry Gallagher; *The Abolition of Marriage* (D.C.: Regnery 1996) p. 63

11 Gayle Rosenwald Smith, Sally Abrahms; *What Every Woman Should Know About Divorce and Custody* (New York: Perigee 2007)

12 Real Detroit Weekly; Interview; *The Rehabilitation of Eminem* May 19th 2009; Accessed Dec 24 2009; http:// www. Real detroitweekly.com/content/article_5329.shtml

13 The New York Times; Article; *Ethnically Ambiguous*; Dec, 28 2003; Accessed May 9, 2009; http://www.nytimes.com/2003/12/28/style/generation-ea-ethnicallyambiguous.html? pagewanted=2

Chapter NINE

1 Elijah Anderson, *Code of the Streets* (New York: Norton 1999) p. 210

2 Nicki Minaj; Video Interview; Accessed February 15, 2010; http://www.hiphopsheartbeat.com/musicvideo.php?vid=bd1c2 3c28

3 Raquel Welch; Article; *It's Sex O'clock in America*; Posted May 9, 2010; Accessed May 11, 2010; http://edition.cnn.com/2010/OPINION/05/07/welch.sex.pill/i ndex.html

4 Nicki Minaj; Interview; Accessed January 6, 2010; http://www.complex.com/GIRLS/Videos/Nicki-Minaj

5 Beyonce Knowles; Interview; Accessed October 6th 2010; http://hellobeautiful.com/your-world/beyonce-named-billboards-woman-of-the-year/

Chapter TEN

1 Drake; Interview; Accessed February 6th, 2010;
http://hoodstarhiphop.com/video/sVRZFUuoVyI/

2 Benjamin Todd Jealous; Interview; *The New NAACP*; Aired on CNN July 18th 2009

3 50 Cent; Interview; September 7th 2007; Accessed July 10 2009; http://hoodstarhiphop.com/video/sVRZFUuoVyI/

4 Bakari Kitwana; *The Hip Hop Generation* (New York: Civitas 2002) p. 105

5 Lupe Fiasco; Interview; Accessed May 15, 2010;
http://www.247hh.com/watch/episode/26

6 Raymond J. Corsini; Danny Wedding; *Current Psychotherapies* (Belmont: Thomson 2008) p. 196 – 99

Chapter ELEVEN

1 Bertrand Russell; *Marriage and Morals*; (New York: Liveright 1957) p. 89

2 http://www.etymonline.com/index.php?term=moral; Accessed May 16, 2010

3 Thomas Harris; *I'm OK--You're OK* (New York: Harper 1969)

4 The Pew Forum; *Many Americans Mix Multiple Faiths*; December 9, 2009; Accessed January 17, 2010; http:// / pew forum.org/Other-Beliefs-and-Practices/Many-Americans-Mix-Multiple-Faiths.aspx

5 Scott B. Rae; *Moral Choices* 2nd Edition (Grand Rapids: Zondervan 2000) p. 81

6Rep. John Sullivan (R) Oklahoma; House Energy subcmte. Cross examination of BP CEO Tony Hayward; June 17, 2010; Aired live: CNN Telecast.

Chapter TWELVE

1 Marty Grothe; *Oxymoronica* (New York: Harper 2004) p. 28

2 Bertrand Russell; *Marriage and Morals*; (New York: Liveright 1957) p. 157

3 CNN.com; How The Wheels Came Off; Transcript; Aired May 29, 2009; http://transcripts.cnn.com/TRANSCRIPTS/0905/29/ec.01.html

4 Today Show; *Intextication*; Aired July 28, 2009

5 CNN.com; Report: *Staffers Watched Porn While Economy Crashed*; April 23, 2010; Accessed April 29, 2010; http://www.cnn.com/2010/POLITICS/04/23/sec.porn/index.html

6 Scott B. Rae; *Moral Choices* 2nd Edition (Grand Rapids: Zondervan 2000) p. 238

7 C.S. Lewis, *Mere Christianity* (San Francisco: Harper 1952) p.95

8 CNBC; *Controversy Over Trojan Condom Ad*; June 19, 2007; http://www.cnbc.com/id/19306576/;

9 *American Experience; Summer of Love; March* 14, 2007; Accessed May 16, 2010; http://www.pbs.org/wgbh /amex / love/filmmore/pt.html

[10] Cornel West; *Democracy Matters* (New York: Penguin 2004) p. 177

Chapter THIRTEEN

[1] Edward T. Welch; *When People are Big and God is Small* (Phillipsburg: P&R 1997) p. 155

[2] Saint Augustine; *Confessions* (London: Penguin 1961) p. 148

[3] Michael Warner; *American Sermons*: Jonathon Edward; *Sinners in the Hands of an Angry God* (New York: Library 1999) p. 354-55

[4] C.S. Lewis; *The Knowledge of the Holy* (San Francisco: Harper 1961) p. 60

[5] C.S. Lewis; *The Chronicles of Narnia: The Lion, The Witch And The Wardrobe* (New York: Harper 1950) p. 80

Chapter FOURTEEN

[1] Dorothy Sayers; *The Lost Tools of Learning*; 1947

[2] Julie Landsman, Chance W. Lewis; *White Teachers Diverse Classrooms* (New York: Stylus 2006) p. 55

The Death of Hip Hop, Marriage & Morals and other
resources from this author are available online at

www.urbanremixproject.com

Also and internationally through:

Createspace.com & Amazon.com

The author is available for speaking engagements; send request
and information to   info@urbanremixproject.com

6724309R0

Made in the USA
Charleston, SC
30 November 2010